THE VELVET GLOVE OF LEADERSHIP IN THE 2020S

LEADERSHIP PRINCIPLES THAT DON'T CHANGE IN A CHANGING WORLD

BY DENNIS E. SMITH

DORRANCE
PUBLISHING CO
EST. 1920
PITTSBURGH, PENNSYLVANIA 15238

Dorrance Publishing Co
585 Alpha Drive
Suite 103
Pittsburgh, PA 15238
Visit our website at *www.dorrancebookstore.com*

ISBN: 979-8-88925-152-1
eISBN: 979-8-88925-652-6

THE VELVET GLOVE OF LEADERSHIP IN THE 2020S

LEADERSHIP PRINCIPLES THAT DON'T CHANGE IN A CHANGING WORLD

The last decades of the 1900s and the first two decades of the 2000s have seen ever increasing changes. Consider these amazing inventions that are so commonplace today and the generations that lived through the remarkable inventions and a singularity called Covid 19.

- The first Apple computer was released in 1976
- **<u>January 1980, the first Digital Native is born</u>**
- **January 1981, the first Gen Y baby is born.**
- The first 8 bit home computer Commodore 64 computer was introduced in January 1982
- January 1, 1983, the communications protocol, Transfer Control Protocol/Internetwork Protocol (TCP/IP), was introduced to the public.
- MCI Communications Corporations introduces the first commercial email service in 1983
- **January 1986, the first Gen X baby turns 21**
- File sharing in email was made possible with the introduction of Multipurpose Internet Mail Extensions (MIME) in 1992
- The first text message was sent on December 3, 1992
- April 30, 1993, the first web browser and editor, "Mesh", was released into the public domain
- **January 1997, the first Gen Z baby is born**
- **January 2002, the first Gen Y baby turns 21**
- June 2007, the first generation iPhone enters the market in the US
- 2010, video conferencing becomes possible with the iPhone 4
- **2011, the first Baby Boomers are eligible to retire at age 65**
- **2018, the first Gen Z baby turns 21**
- December 2019, Covid 19 is identified for the first time in Wuhan China

- March 15 2020, states in the US begin to implement shut-down due to Covid 19
- January 2023, Covid deaths approach 1,100,000 in the US and an unprecedented exodus of working age adults from the workforce continues.

Just the tip of the iceberg, but it is easy to see that the old norms have left the building and whatever the new normal is has not completely settled in. And in the middle of all of this, companies still have to produce, families need to be sheltered and fed, and new leaders get to assume the mantle of leadership in interesting times. Lots and lots of change in almost every facet of life, but leaders are still leaders and the fundamentals of leadership still hold.

Purpose of this Book

The timeline in the introduction laid out the pace of change in technology with a few social milestones for contest, but consider that a person born in 1910 may have experienced horse and buggy transportation, yet, at age 59, saw Neil Armstrong walk on the moon. They also lived through two world wars, saw the nuclear age begin, and the first human organ transplants.

The pace of change may be faster, the technology may be different, but one thing remains and that is the desperate need for good leaders that understand the need for inspirational leadership. So in the broadest sense, this book is about you.

This small book is a mirror of sorts that you can view yourself, in the context of the art and science of leadership. The hope is that you will find some new skill and some timeless truth that helps you understand that, regardless of the current circumstances and technogolgy, the pace of change, and whatever crazy next new thing the world has to offer, the responsibility of leadership does not change. Beyond the brief discussion of the art and science of leadership, the hope is that the picture of intentional leadership comes into focus.

Those that stand up to the self-examination and, over time, develop into an effective and intentional leader will be in high demand.

How to use this book

This book is really two books in one: Part one examines leadership and management imperatives, or the art of leadership along with leadership and management skills required to succeed today in the world of work. Although not all leaders are managers and not all managers are leaders, there is enough overlap that this book will use the term leader throughout for simplicity.

The intent of the book is to keep Part 1 brief and to the point and a quick read and Part 2 is intended to be a tool box for leaders, available when needed.

You will notice **text or hyperlinks** in various places in Part 1 that point the reader directly to a chapter or topic in the leaders tool box (Part 2) for additional information, when and if the reader chooses to drill down into a particular topic. In addition there are links to YouTube for brief videos on the more complex topics.

The torch of leadership is being passed to technically competent individuals; this book is an attempt to pass along the softer skills of leadership and hopefully bring value to the reader.

TABLE OF CONTENTS

Part 1: Leadership Imperatives and Leadership Skills

PART 1:

LEADERSHIP IMPERATIVES AND LEADERSHIP SKILLS

CHAPTER 1
LEADERSHIP IMPERATIVES

Leadership in the 2020s may be especially challenging given the technological and human turmoil of the last few years and decades, but one thing remains the same; there are key leadership imperatives that remain relevant. Consider the important topics below and how closely they mesh up with how you perceive yourself and how others may perceive you.

ACTIVE LISTENING

The leadership art of active listening; the learned ability where the listener focuses entirely on the speaker. No answering the phone, responding to a text, or thinking about golf later in the day. Good listeners ask questions to draw out the truth as best they can, understanding that subordinates may be afraid to come out and say what the issue may be, particularity if the issue is with the leader themselves.

This is a difficult skill to build and may require a pivot from old habits. Most of us tend to quickly form an opinion very quickly and, in doing so, formulate a response even before the other person stops talking. We all tend to make judgements based on personal appearance, language skills, position within the organization and more (page

96, understand self and others); unfortunately the bias of those judgements tend to overshadow the information being shared.

Active listening should include clarifying questions (page 78, tell back explanation) in order to get to the meat of the conversation. Consider that subordinates may be reluctant to clearly state a particular issue due to fear of reprisal and it may take some effort to drill down to the true nature of the conversation.

Active listening should include an opportunity for the listener to "tell back" (page 78, tell back explanation), or restate what the listener heard with the purpose allowing the sender of the message to validate what the listener heard.

Keep in mind that verbal communication is only one aspect of listening and that body language may send a completely different message than what is said. Good eye contact is a positive signal that both parties are listening. Head nods, good posture, leaning in, and positive facial expressions like a smile are also a good indicator of open communication. Negative body language of poor posture or slouching, avoiding eye contact, crossed arms, fidgeting, and negative facial expressions are warning signals that the leader needs to hit the pause button and attempt to understand what barriers may be interrupting the effort to communicate, (page 71, communicate well or nothing else matters).

Just a word of caution, different genders may see and hear things differently than you. This certainly makes leadership of mixed teams more interesting and demands that leadership develop, as best they can, the different perspectives of those they lead. When in doubt, invite a team member of the same gender as the person you are meeting with, to observe and share insight as appropriate.

UNDERSTANDING THE ISSUES

Leaders must understand the issue or event at work in any given circumstance. This art of leadership is one that attempts to look at issues from different perspectives, and takes the time, when time allows, to analyze a problem (page 49, problem solving tools) to formulate an action.

The challenge for leaders to understand is that issues or problems or emergencies are seldom one-dimensional, and may span several departments or teams over which the leader may have no authority, or which may not be addressed in the policies and procedures (page 39, creating lanes) of the company or department.

Emergent situations are particularly challenging in that an issue may be unfolding in a way that it may not be recognized as an emergency until some time passes. In those instances, the default for most leaders is to correlate the unfolding event with a similar event and to correlate the response to how a response was rendered in a similar, but not identical, event and this is human nature.

The challenge to the leader is to slow down and understand what they are seeing before coming to a conclusion and developing a response.

COACHING AND ASSISTING OTHERS

All leaders and all team members, and in this case the use of the word *all* is appropriate, will from time to time make mistakes and errors, occasionally at great cost to the organization. Successful leaders are those that recognize that most mistakes are learning opportunities, and work to help others learn from their experience. Sometimes the most valuable team members are those that have learned valuable life lessons from an event they would just as soon forget.

Coaching, while similar in some aspects to counseling (page 51, the fear free environment), typically is more orientated to helping a team member to come to their own conclusion by asking questions, encouraging the team member to develop ideas for consideration, working to help the team member connect the current issue or problem to a previous experience, working with the team member to help remove any blinders and expand their thinking, and helping the team member come to a conclusion that is beneficial to both the team and the team member.

Coaching falls in the hard work category of a leader. Assisting with a particular task or training for a certain task or activity may be easier, but there are some instances where coaching, training, or counseling (page 36, red ants and tall poppies) do not work even with repeated effort and hard choices must be made, (page 34, firing), and the decision must be made to part ways.

BUILDING A RATIONAL CASE FOR DECISIONS

If we lived in a static world without change, would leaders really be necessary? Fortunately this is a moot question since change, like the change in the few short decades in the introductory timeline, is constant. In fact the pace of change may be increasing with every passing year, so how does a leader build a case for the decision they make to address the dynamic external and internal forces that drive the need for change making decisions?

The rational model of decision making (Kinicki and Kreitner 2003, pg.178-179) would have a leader follow a four-step process to build a case for making a particular decision: identifying the problem (page 49, problem solving tools), generating potential solutions, selecting the best possible solution, and then implementing and evaluating the effectiveness of the solution, (page 41, operating in control).

The rational model tends to be appropriate when all the facts are known and there is a clear cut "best choice solution" to the issue. Unfortunately, it is rare for all the facts to be gathered or time and resources may constrain the decision maker driving them to an alternative decision making process, or normative decision making, based on limited information, heuristics (rule of thumb shortcuts to processing data), and choosing a "good" (Kinicki and Kreitner 2003, pg.179-181) solution rather than waiting for all the pieces of the problem to fall into place before acting.

The initial step of identifying the problem remains a critical piece of the process so that the proposed decision addresses the root of a given issue rather than the various symptoms that may be more obvious; however, in a fast moving environment, leaders may be limited to facts that tend to be more readily available and not the entire universe of fact that could be gathered if there were no constraints. The caution for leaders building a case for decisions, is that there may be a "better" solution that is not being considered. Voltaire once said, "The perfect is the enemy of the good," making the point that a good decision that satisfies a certain situation is better than be paralyzed in decision making while waiting on every last fact (page 71, ethics and leadership).

Once a root cause has been identified based on the available information, then the leader begins to use the filters of past experiences and availability of solutions. In this particular approach, leaders tend to remember solutions that have worked before and to attempt to apply a variant of those solution to the current situation. The second filter leaders often use is only considering what is readily available to solve the problem, which tends to limit potential solutions. The final filter is the probability filter that assigns the potential for a certain event to happen or to be changed based on how past events unfolded.

Bringing in key staff in the problem solving process may bring different perspectives and experiences that, even with incomplete information or facts, can lead to a "good" solution and assist in building a reasonable case for a given solution.

Other problem solving models exist, but are generally variations on those in the above paragraphs. The most important consideration for a leader is action on an issue. Inaction or a wavering approach to building a case for a particular decision, is demoralizing to staff and disappointing to senior leaders. Secondly, the decision must be communicated (page 71, communicate well or nothing else matters) with the three C's of communication: clarity, confidence, and conviction.

BUILDING UP AND ENCOURAGING OTHERS

This particular art of leadership sounds similar to coaching but has characteristics of its own and for our purpose in this discussion may best be called sponsorship, although mentoring is a very large factor as well. (Kinicki and Kreitner 2003 pg. 36)

Sponsorship starts from day one with a new hire (page 31, hiring), or when new relationships form with changes in leadership (page 42, types and formations of teams). Sponsorship, in this larger context, is a leader charting a course for a subordinate that will integrate (page 63, corporate and team culture) the new member into the team or organization (page 38, so you have a team, now what), as well as expanding the depth and breadth of knowledge and experience the individual brings to the team.

Sponsors encourage the development of the individual within the organization and make opportunities for the individual to build relationships with peers within the organization to better understand how to navigate in a new assignment. Sponsors also should look outside the organization to professional associations that may provide technical education and network opportunities that may be of benefit. If a professional organization is not a possibility, then the sponsor should consider the possibility of encouraging membership in a volunteer or civic organization, or continuing education, that may help build a particular skill set that would benefit the individual and in a larger context, the organization. The key word is *encourage* as any forced relationships are likely to not go so well.

The challenge for the sponsor is to understand that the more interaction the new team member has with their peers and with leadership, the stronger the bond and more effective the relationship. The same holds true for the interaction between the leader and the team member.

Many leaders are reluctant to invest this much effort in an individual with the thought that the more complete and well rounded the person becomes, the more likely they are to leave for other opportunities. The choice, whether it is said out loud or not, is to keep a low performing team member on the team or to build a team member up where they are more valuable to team and possibly a competitor.

RECOGNITION AND REWARDS

Few things, in the business world, are more satisfying than success, but success is usually hard won and not as frequent as one would like. When a successful conclusion to a task, a project, a banner year, or whatever the opportunity, it is important for the leader to share the glow of success and provide opportunities for the entire team to enjoy that moment. If some team member has made a particularly significant contribution to team success, they deserve some special recognition.

The military is particularly good at visible recognition of achievement. Look at any military dress uniform and the row upon row of colorful ribbons that denote some special achievement or act of courage. Typically this recognition happens in close relationship to the time of the event or act. The lesson here is to recognize team members as soon as is practical before the shine of the moment passes (page 63, corporate and team culture-observable artifacts). This does not preclude a follow up in the company newsletter or a post in social media.

Confident leaders recognize that success of their team or of an individual on the team, reflects well on the leader.

CHAPTER 2
SKILLS FOR
SUCCESSFUL LEADERS

Skill sets for successful leaders (Kinicki and Kreitner 2003 pg. 8)

In Chapter 1 we looked at imperatives for leaders. In this chapter we drill down into the mechanics of working with high performing teams with practical advice on specific leadership and management skills required to draw out the best from each team member. Many of these skills address the ability of leaders at every level to take what may be a complex plan crossing all departments in an organization (page 56, strategic planning) and breaking those very large concepts and objectives into understandable terms for the leader and their subordinates and then creates a plan to contribute to the overall success of the organization.

CLARIFYING GOALS AND OBJECTIVES FOR THE TEAM

Note the use of the term "clarifies goals and objectives". High performing organizations usually develop or update strategic plans on a regular basis. When the organizations plan is updated, or when performance in relation to the plan is measured, leaders across the entire spectrum must ask the question, what does this mean to my team and what do we need to concentrate on to be judged successful and how do I communicate these potentially new requirements to the team?

Often an objective established by an organization requires several different departments within the organization, each to be successful with a certain piece of the larger plan. The work to accomplish any part of a larger plan should be crafted in as small of tasks as possible that build upon each other to result in overall success. Identifying the building blocks that make up a given task allows leaders to quickly spot a task that may require a midcourse correction which is so much easier to address than waiting until a the task is due to be complete, then discovering the task will not complete on time.

ENCOURAGES PARTICIPATION, UPWARD COMMUNICATION, AND SUGGESTIONS

Goals and objectives require that tactics be developed by all leaders, ideally with input from staff that contribute to the success of the organization. Effective leaders encourage input from the team to assist in understanding what a new or modified tactic may mean to team performance. Team participation can help identify necessary changes to policies and procedures or what new tool may be required to meet changed tactics.

Teams are often made up of individuals with diverse backgrounds and these various viewpoints hopefully will also provide different perspectives for any given problem. The challenge is to moderate this input from various individuals without charging down different paths and loosing track of the ultimate goal of identifying and completing a certain task. Certain ground rules have to be established regarding how the group interacts; for example, no personal attacks are allowed, others time will be honored with meetings starting and stopping on time (page 83, effective meetings) and agreement that the group will accept the outcome of the discussions.

The ultimate goal for leaders is to come to a "we" conclusion rather than a top down directive.

PLANS AND ORGANIZES FOR ORDERLY WORK FLOW

No organization has unlimited resources. There is almost always more work to accomplish than the resources available, so leaders must prioritize demands based on the team's current capabilities. Some tasks may need to be outsourced, some automated, and some deferred until a later date. Expectations both up and downstream of the leader must be managed and definitions of success established.

Teams have scheduled work, routine administrative tasks, and emergencies they must respond to from time to time. With the flood of demands on a typical day, team focus can easily shift off of those important tasks (page 93, time management). A common complaint is that there are simply not enough hours during the day to get everything done. There may be truth to that particular complaint, but the bottom line is that it really does not matter. Goals must be met, and critical tasks accomplished.

The key phrase here is "plans and organizes". Leaders may decide that a "simple" task may not need oversight, but often those simple tasks, when not completed, become a bigger issue. The safest concept for a leader is to understand there really is no such thing as a simple task. Leaders should consider how to capture milestone achievement on a regular basis. This can be in any number of ways, but a powerful tool for special project or activities that have multiple milestones to be met is Microsoft Project.

Leaders must be willing to step in at critical times to assist the team where possible and work with the team to keep the main effort in focus. Just as importantly, leaders are obligated to keep upper leadership informed, and more importantly, never bring a problem to upper leadership without a proposed solution. Communication, delivered without delay, both up and down, is critical. Bad news, in particular, is best exposed as soon as the issue is understood and reporting methods put in place for team member to validate that a particular assignment has been completed.

HAS TECHNICAL AND ADMINISTRATIVE EXPERIENCE TO ANSWER ORGANIZATION AND TEAM QUESTIONS

The leader is expected to have a certain skill set in order to manage a team. This does not necessarily mean that the leader is expected to be an expert in every task the team performs: that may not be practical in highly technical teams with a variety of skill sets, but the leader should be familiar enough to identify when team performance is not to an acceptable standard.

More often than not, new leaders, and sometimes even seasoned leaders, will find themselves in a leadership position over a team with completely unfamiliar tasks or skill sets. Knowing what you know and knowing what you do not know is essential in these circumstances. Once the leader has a firm grasp on what they do not know, they can have the technical experts on the team train them (while this may seem to diminish the leader to admit a lack of knowledge in a certain area, the opposite is more often true where the team respects this type of action), or there may be mentors within the organization that may be a good source of knowledge.

Where the organizational knowledge does not exist, the leader has other options, usually through trade organizations, contracted experts, or through classes or courses offered through local universities.

One excellent example was a medical doctor who was tapped to lead a practice of several pediatricians. This MD was obviously well educated, but knew what he knew and what he did not know and made a choice to return to school for an MBA in order to meet the expectations of his peers. The takeaway from this example is the MD selected to lead a group practice was humble enough to admit that he needed to know more for the team to be successful.

An important takeaway is not to become complacent and stop learning something new every day. Retiring in place does no favors to the organization, the leader or the leader's team. Another important takeaway for leaders is to know what they know and know what they do not know. The decision then is to gain additional knowledge like the MD or whether to reach out to, and lean on others with expertise when needed. It's okay to acknowledge, "I don't know, but I'll find out."

FACILITATES WORK THROUGH TEAM BUILDING, TRAINING, COACHING, AND SUPPORT

The team leader must continually keep their finger on the pulse of the team in order to recognize when and where training and coaching opportunities surface. An example may be a new software program introduced to the team; this is an obvious opportunity to bring in vendor experts for team training. Other opportunities may not be so obvious, and the leader may need to go through a problem solving exercise (addressed in this book) to determine the root cause of reduced team performance and provide the training, coaching and support necessary to bring the team back to peak performance.

Interestingly, coaching may be the most important aspect of leadership for the newest generation of employees. They may be very comfortable with the concept of coaching and accept that aspect of leadership without much pushback.

CONTROLS DETAILS WITHOUT BEING OVERBEARING

The days of expendable employees, if they ever existed, are long past. This does not mean, however, that shoddy work or failure to meet various milestones can be accepted.

If the planning, problem solving, and agreement on responsibilities are done properly, then leaders can concentrate on the details. Again, the team members should agree on the details that fall for them to complete. If that agreement is a yes in public and a no in private, then the leaders have a completely different issue to deal with.

Controlling details is where policies and procedures come into play. In addition, the special projects should result in a step-by-step plan with measurable results. If the team members have agreed to follow the policies and procedures, or the specific tasks assigned to them on a special project, then it should not be a burden to either the leader or team member to provide an update on their performance at any given time.

The key takeaway for controlling details is that those details and assignments must be clear and un-ambiguous. Questions need to be addressed, as much as is possible, regarding the details and then when additional issues arise, leaders have a critical duty to bring an answer to the individual or team as soon as possible so as not to interrupt the work flow.

APPLIES REASONABLE PRESSURE FOR GOAL ACCOMPLISHMENT

This skill overlaps with the skill of *controls details* without being overbearing, but there are subtle differences.

For both skill sets, team members need to believe that leadership understands the distractors that each of them face every day. Team members that believe their leader is working to remove obstacles may be less resentful when that same leader presses on the details.

Leaders must clearly state what details they will check to ensure there are no surprises. There is an old adage that "employees do what the boss checks", and there is a lot of truth in that. Tell the team up front what leadership will check on and regularly make those checks with the knowledge of the entire team. When results lag, seek input from the team regarding corrective action, and finally take decisive action.

Positive reinforcement is almost always better, so leadership could provide a team lunch when an important milestone is met, or use company resources to announce the success of the team from time to time.

One very interesting tool leaders may consider is a partnering agreement for special projects. This may be developed at the kickoff meeting for a project where the participants are given a final opportunity to clear the air of lingering questions and concerns. The partnering agreement then codifies the expectations for success and states how the team interacts with one another and when and how missed expectations may be addressed. Assuming the entire team agrees to the terms of this non-binding agreement, everyone signs the documents and copies provided to all.

EMPOWERS AND DELEGATES KEY DUTIES TO OTHERS WHILE MAINTAINING GOAL CLARITY AND COMMITMENT

The days of showing up to work an eight-hour day and following orders are past. Employees today are typically interested in the "why" of the work and how it really contributes to the organization.

In 1960 a gentleman by the name of David McGregor wrote a book called *The Human Side of Enterprise* (Kinicki and Kreitner 2003 pg. 11-12) and proposed a new theory of management, called theory Y, to replace the old, top down, theory X. Even newer theories exist, but Theory Y remains relevant.

Theory Y states that work is a natural part of human existence, rather than something to be avoided. Theory Y proposed that people are capable of self-direction and self-control if they are committed to objectives, and tend to become committed if they are rewarded (monetary rewards are always important, but money without personal recognition does not build commitment). Further the theory proposes that the typical employee can accept and actually looks for responsibility in their job and has the ingenuity and creativity to do so.

Leaders that train employees and allow a reasonable degree of autonomy and authority will quickly identify those on the team that respond positively. Leaders must always be aware that ultimate responsibility for team performance cannot be delegated, but rests with the leader.

The challenge for leaders is to recognize which tasks can be delegated and those that must firmly remain in their control. Generally, the more routine the task, the easier to delegate. There is a direct correlation with another phenomenon where team members may attempt to bring one of their tasks or issues they should be expected to deal with and put it back on the shoulders of the team leader. Leaders should be aware and recognize when this is attempted and understand they can quickly be buried in work that is better done by others.

RECOGNIZES GOOD PERFORMANCE WITH REWARDS AND POSITIVE REINFORCEMENT

As stated earlier, positive reinforcement should be the default method to motivate employees and may be appropriate to help shift team or company culture when necessary.

One real life example of shifting culture using rewards and positive reinforcements was driven by necessity. My construction company experienced a period when Workman's Compensation claims had driven insurance premiums to an unsustainable level. Working with the insurance company, we developed a solution where we would pay each employee a silver dollar for every day worked without a lost time injury. Payment would only be made if their crew members were also injury free for that time period.

Payments were made at the end of every calendar quarter and all 85 employees were brought in on company time to participate in the payout. On the first "safety day" payout there were almost 6,000 silver dollars stacked on the table, which was an impressive sight. Every employee except for one crew of 7, were paid. The crew that was not paid had experienced a lost time injury and therefore not eligible for the three month payout. The peer pressure on the crew that did not receive their silver dollars was significant and from that day forward, the crew looked out for one another and called out unsafe practices immediately.

Safety Days worked and, for an investment of less than $24,000 we were able to reduce insurance policy cost well over $100,000. Budgets are always a consideration, but there may be a line item that can be converted, with permission from senior leaders, that may be redeployed to shift team or company behavior.

PROVIDES HONEST AND CONSTRUCTIVE FEEDBACK

Sometimes things do not seem to go so well. Leaders and team members are human and have to deal not only with work performance but all those things that happen in the other sixteen hours of the day, and it is incumbent upon the leader to be open to recognizing when performance begins to slip.

Leaders must take the time to understand, as best as possible, what the contributing factors are for reduced performance. Job related disruptions with other team members, or from a failed plan or a defective tool are relatively easy to address since most of the pieces are under the control of the leader. Outside problems like divorce or illness of a family member are obviously outside the leader's control, but simply understanding the issues may lead to a workable temporary solution to help the team member through a difficult time. The team member has to decide for themselves how much they will share with their leader and other team members, but in a high functioning team, it can be surprising how much the team will step in to ease the burden of one of their members.

In 2022 several new performance issues began to surface, one of which is quiet quitting. Quiet quitting is simply where the team member has begun retirement in place and performance within the team begins to deteriorate. Another interesting attribute that has begun to display is withholding expertise from others (page 29, people, why we do what we do). Yet another is an addiction to screens where phone use by the employee goes well beyond that of job-related necessity. None of this is really new, it simply has a new name, since, with the exceptions of addiction to screens, and human behavior really hasn't changed that much for a very long time. The addiction to screens is really just another addiction like those that have come before and, for the most part, continue to exist to tamp down human potential.

Failure for leadership to act may damage the team performance and drag down otherwise high performers and this is the time for honest and constructive feedback after enough of the information is in for a reasonable assessment of the situation.

Feedback should be non-threatening and should address the known issues and attempt to discover if there are other issues that have not been discovered. Other chapters in this book discuss documentation of constructive feedback (page 88, managing conflict), and that should be considered. If the leader expects the discussion to be particularly difficult, it may be beneficial to have a third party from HR or another department leader, sit in as a witness of the feedback. Old fashioned guidance would be that if the team member to be counseled is of the opposite sex, then the door stays open or a third party be present to guard against the image of impropriety.

Finally, feedback delayed will not make the situation better. When the facts are in hand and an attempt has been made to learn the less obvious issues, it is time for leadership to act.

A LOOK AHEAD AT THE LEADERS TOOL BOX

Over the course of Part 1, we have looked at a variety of topics for consideration that may be of some value to new leaders. Embedded in many of the imperatives and skills were notes to jump to a certain page or hypertext that offered the reader an opportunity to drill down into more complex topics, but not all of the chapters in Part 2 were referenced. In particular there are discussions on Total Quality Management (page 49, more about TQM) to enable the leader to begin to identify built in obstacles to performance and how to correct those issues. Strategic planning is discussed with the purpose of familiarizing the reader with where their responsibilities may be in the planning process (page 56, strategic planning).

In Part 2 there is a discussion of personality types (page 96, understand yourself and others) provided so that the leader can better understand themselves and others. There are also chapters on hiring, specifics on documenting performance counseling, and dismissing a team member that misses the mark (page 29, People, why we do what we do).

We discussed ethics (page 61, ethics and leadership) and the development of a team or company culture (page 63, corporate and team culture) in order to establish the guiding principles for the organization; principals that underlie every decision made.

Communication (page 71, communicate well or nothing else matters), effective meetings (page 83, conducting effective meetings), negotiating skills (page 86, negotiations, part of leadership), and conflict management (page 88, Managing conflict) are discussed with some practical examples presented for consideration.

There is also a section that looks at successful and failed leaders (page 103, heroes and goats) in history with the purpose of generating curiosity in what works and what does not. The good examples are called heroes as the concept of having a personal hero to emulate can help to shape leadership styles. I have also included some personal observations and a short wrap up of the concept of the Velvet Glove of Leadership

Finally, and possibly more important of all, we looked at work life balance looked at work/life balance (page 90, balancing work, self, and home), and general time management (page 93, time management).

My hope is that there has been a nugget or two of value that you can use. After over 56 years of being "responsible and in charge", I know that I wish I had this insight earlier. The construction company that I was CEO and owner, along with a handful of other partners, fell apart because I did not know or chose to ignore some of these principals. A company with a $2 million dollar payroll and 82 employees was gone after only 18 months, when I was invited to leave, because I fell short.

It was a painful experience, but that pain led me to another career in health-care at a mid-sized hospital and then on to a position as a national leader where I met and worked with some outstanding leaders and team members. Overall it has been a great ride and it has been a privilege to have led a lifetime of leadership.

I wish you good fortune and satisfaction in your endeavors.

PART 2

THE LEADERS TOOLBOX

Table of Contents Part 2

Link to YouTube videos for more information
https://www.youtube.com/@SCSLLC

PEOPLE-WHY WE DO WHAT WE DO
A NOTE FOR CONSIDERATION

The section below speaks of leaders and team member or employees, however not all relationships fit that particular characterization. Leaders can have responsibility in volunteer organizations, clubs, or any number of relationships that humans conceive of from time to time. The reader will need to determine what applies to their particular situation.

Volunteer organizations are great training camps for leaders. When a leader is proficient such that they can get good results from a team that could walk out the door at any time, then that is an accomplishment that translates well to other endeavors. Some companies, when looking to fill leadership positions, pay particular attention to experience in leading volunteer groups. Never sell the leadership of a group of volunteers short; it can be very challenging and very rewarding. In fact the large healthcare company I worked for was very interested if I had a chance to lead in a volunteer organization and what my experiences were in that position.

At the end of the day, the relationship between the leader and the led can be as simple as this: treat others as you would like to be treated. You may have read that somewhere, and it sounds easy, but so few really do that. Put a sign on the wall and do whatever it takes to remember this first rule of leadership.

SPAN OF CONTROL

From the beginning of human history, examples exist where one person was given responsibility to motivate, encourage and lead others toward a common goal. Over time an element of leadership known as "span of control", emerged as a most basic tool of leadership. Historically, a leader's span of control generally would be from seven to ten subordinates with that number decreasing for complex tasks or missions or increasing for rote tasks that may be simple or repetitive.

The Roman Armies that conquered the world are one example of span of control in their organization. The book of Exodus in the Christian Bible has examples of how the Israelites were organized for their 40 year journey in the desert are another. Fortunately for us, conquering the world or endless wandering in the wilderness are not something we need to worry about. But we do need to understand what is a reasonable number for leader and their team.

The days of marching into battle in a Roman Legion are past, but the lesson for leaders regarding span of control remains. Look at large organizations where the leader may be a President or CEO with a handful of Vice Presidents answering up. Each VP may have four or five Directors of various departments answering up. Each Director may have three or four or more Managers that answer up. Each Manager may have one or more Supervisors over a team answering up.

The nomenclature used in any given organization may vary and may be structured in a very rigid and vertical organizational chart or less rigid and more horizontal format. Regardless, the theme of "span of control", envisioned by the Romans two thousand years ago, will likely be present in any high performing organization.

The benefit of structure allows everyone in the organization to understand where they fit, and from whom their instructions should come and to whom they report. Without structure, messages may become muddled, subordinates may be bombarded by demands from a number of folks higher up in the organizational chart and become demoralized by the cascade of conflicting demands and the dissemination of the organizations goals is more difficult. The same structure should provide a known environment for the most valuable asset of any organization, its employees.

Very small start-up companies are very different from the corporate world and one person may wear a number of hats in the company. This is completely normal in an entrepreneurial society and the challenge for the leader in this type of environment is to recognize when a more formal structure needs to be implemented. Many leaders in small organizations may never be to the point when the span of control becomes an issue and there is nothing inherently wrong with leadership in a very small organization, but the danger is the leader can be consumed by the many various rolls they play and burn out.

Organizational structures vary widely, but two common types of structure can be characterized as "flat" or "hierarchal". I have had the opportunity to operate in both and neither are inherently good or bad. In my experience, flat organizations tend to have lower management cost, may be more nimble in their approach to change, but can tend to be a little confusing for team member to navigate. Span of control in these organizations can tend to be large with a high leader to team member ratio.

Hierarchal organizations tend to have structured lines of communication, may have a smaller span of control, tend to have a higher management cost as there are leaders for smaller numbers of team members. These types of organizations may not be as nimble and adapt to incremental change as a flat organization, but in emergency situations, may react rapidly if necessary.

So what works today? Even in the world of instant communication, a span of "control" of 7-10 could be considered. "Control" may be better defined as the reasonable number of team members that can be coached and developed by any given leader. Leaders with a staff of highly educated or trained team members with similar tasks, can function well in a flater organization and a high span of control. Leaders with team members with a broader skill set or that may encounter complex and novel tasks, may require a lower span of control to address emergent issues.

HIRING

Hiring for a small company is much more straightforward than the processes put in place in the corporate world, however there are nuggets of value in considering some of the elements involved in hiring in the corporate world. Regardless, this is an attempt to examine the Human side of Human Resource Management-something that tends to get lost when more people become involved in the process.

First, Human Resource Management is very complex and those that specialize in HR may have, and likely should have, undergraduate and/or graduate degrees in the subject. Labor laws can be very complex and employee relations in open shop or union shop environments can be very different. Further, the company may likely have an entire department to assist in recruiting and developing human capital. This book does not do a deep dive into the complexities of HR, but rather looks at a few of the issues for leaders to consider when bringing new employees into the team. In specific questions on labor law, discipline, promotions and so forth, the leader at any given level should consult with professionals or the company HR team or trusted legal counsel, to better avoid the pitfalls that can arise from time to time.

One of the most important tasks of a leader at any level is to hire competent subordinates. The challenge is that very talented people are in demand and may be poached by competitors after investing time to train and mentor these individuals. On the other hand, hiring less talented people may result in a lower performing organization and more effort on the leader to accomplish the tasks at hand. So what's the right answer?

Best practice is to hire the best talent you can afford, train them in the specifics for the position they are in and grant them the autonomy, within the established standards and procedures, to operate. Nothing will drive talented people away more than micro-management.

Well written job descriptions are a must in order to clarify expectations, both up and down, but job descriptions can also be written so restrictively that qualified people are eliminated before they even have an opportunity to apply.

In today's hiring world, larger organizations often depend on computer algorithms to sift through applicants for interviews. Determining educational requirements and experience may be more of an art than science and if the educational or experience requirements are very rigid, then qualified people may be eliminated too soon. The challenge is to look for equivalent knowledge and experience and to write the job description to allow for some degree of judgement in the hiring process. The danger in too loose of a job description is there may be legal issues that could surface later, so time spent detailing the work to be performed and understanding what similar experience and education may be acceptable for the position.

Generally speaking, good leaders like to find people that may have a skill set as good, or better, than their own. It is very difficult for a leader to be proficient in every task for which they may be responsible, so the best approach is to find staff that collectively have more expertise than any single person on the team.

BEHAVIORAL BASED INTERVIEWS

Leaders should always listen carefully to references a potential employee may supply, assuming the hiring process reaches that point. Pay particular attention to what the prospect says and doesn't say. Possibly use hypothetical circumstances to see how the prospect reacts, as an effort to understand how the prospect dealt with demanding circumstances in the past. The question should be crafted with terms like "have you ever had to ....?" and if the answer is no, then drill deeper to determine if there was similar event they had to address. The effort here is to understand how the new team member will likely react to events on your team.

In today's world, most references like to be circumspect with answers regarding a former employee or co-worker simply because a candid answer that costs a potential new hire the opportunity can lead to legal action. The opposite side of that coin is for the leader to be cautious and balance truth with the ever present potential for legal action.

Once a new hire is in place, the job of the leader begins with an orientation into the organization, education on standard procedures, insuring knowledge of the various relationships in the organization. Typically there is a grace period for the new hire to integrate into the team and if there is any doubt, leadership must make a critical go/no go decision prior to the end of the grace period.

SAFETY

Leader's most critical Human Resource task is insuring the safety of their people. Their second most critical task is ensuring the safety of their people.

Every leader should know the various OSHA requirements that may apply to their team and continually share that information with team members. Safety Data Sheets for every chemical the team may encounter must be on hand and understood by the entire team, and an environment of safety must surround everyone on the team, including outside vendors. Many businesses have specific rules and regulations, in addition to OSHA that must be understood and implemented. It is incumbent on the leader to know and understand the regulatory environment and to develop an eye for safety.

Anyone that violates safety regulations and endangers themselves or other team members may be immediately counseled or terminated if the offence warrants. Habitual noncompliance, even by the most skilled or most senior, cannot be tolerated. Period

FIRING

Firing is an unpleasant task, but necessary from time to time. Larger organizations usually have a graduated discipline plan that must be followed to the letter from the initial counseling all the way to terminating the employee. Leaders in small organizations are often left to themselves when the time comes for an employee to leave, but there are still very important things to do when the time comes.

First and most important is documentation. The documentation should follow the company process, where one exists, and where there is no policy, it is still important to record the events surrounding the decision to fire.

Some situations may require immediate dismissal such as an egregious violation of regulatory requirements, a serious safety violation, an unlawful act or some other infraction. Even in those events, it may be a good practice to send the employee home for the day to allow a cooling off period for the leader to consider the proper course of action. Even a verbal reprimand must be documented and if the leader determines it is time for the employee to go, every action and every word should be captured. It is always best to have the employee sign the termination document, but often that does not happen. At the very least, the leader must capture everything surrounding the discipline or actual firing in <u>contemporaneous notes</u>, meaning the notes are captured at the time of the infraction or termination. These notes usually have legal status and can be validated by sending a hard copy to the author of the notes in an envelope that will then be stamped by the postal service, and mailed back to the leader to be kept, unopened, until such a time as it may be needed in legal proceedings. The same thing can be accomplished by emailing the documents to oneself, one's attorney, or some other third party that can retrieve the documents if necessary.

If possible, have a third party present to witness the transaction just in case the firing results in legal action.

Many times, the individual being terminated knows that the time is coming and there is no legal follow-up. In some cases, the leader may offer a termination package, sometimes specified by HR, to ease the transition for the employee. This, of course, depends on the seriousness of the infraction, or infractions driving the termination.

The most important thing for the leader to remember is that every step on from a beginning verbal counseling to termination must be recorded and the cause of the termination be clear to anyone on the outside looking. Secondly, a common error is to wait too long. Failure to act in a timely manner can have long reaching impact. It is amazing how much employees know and learn from observing their leaders. If an employee is allowed to falsify time cards, steal from the company, constantly undermining leadership, and more, the leader can count on the fact that everyone else on the team will know, possibly even before the leader. Failure to act decisively may have a chilling effect on other employees causing a general dissatisfaction and impacting performance across the board. What good employee could possibly want to work in an organization where leaderships allows bad behavior? Decisive action, even in private behind closed doors, will find its way to the water cooler and, if the action is warranted and fair, the organization will be the better for it.

Leaders in companies with Union employees may have a standard process established by the Union that must be followed. Regardless of non-union or union environment, follow any established procedures and seek legal advice if necessary.

RED ANTS AND TALL POPPIES

Inevitably, a Red Ant will make its way into every organization. Red Ants are those people that love to stir the pot with subversive comments or actions. Sometimes this behavior is very difficult to observe as Red Ant may be very good at concealing their activities, this may be what is known as a "passive, aggressive" behavior.

Red Ant behavior can be simple gossip or actual sabotage and the most troubling aspect of the Red Ant is the effect on other employees. First, most of the Red Ant's peers do not want to be the one who brings this person to the attention of leadership. Second, there may be a leadership bias against this type of information and a reluctance to take any action without concrete proof. The most important thing a leader can do for their team is to monitor the team on a regular basis to attempt to detect, in Star Wars terminology, a disturbance in the force. Leaders have to pay attention and if a certain uneasiness starts to develop, that is a danger ahead sign that cannot be ignored.

As with any underperforming employee, document every indicator of a problem and capture those notes as described earlier in the section on firing. Red Ants usually do not go quietly and any misstep in their dismissal will return to haunt leadership.

Tall poppies, on the other hand, are not necessarily disruptors in the organization. If you imagine a beautiful field of Poppies in bloom, the eye immediately is drawn to those Poppy plants that stand tall over all the other Poppies several inches. Farmers may cut these outliers from their fields just to maintain a uniform gene pool of Poppy plants.

Tall Poppies are those in the organization that work to stand out and be noticed for the next promotion, or to achieve some special recognition. Again, not a bad thing, but human nature crops in and the peers in the group may resent that extra, over and above the required level of production. The peer group may begin to tamp down the overachievers, and while this is not as serious as the sabotage of the Red Ant, it is still a disturbance in the force that needs to be recognized so that a perceptive leader can carefully work to keep the Tall Poppy from discouragement, and the rest of the staff from a simmering dislike of anything that upsets the dynamic of the group.

An encouraging word, in a private setting, or a formal mentoring plan may be considered. Team building exercises for the entire team may help to reduce any simmering resentment that may exist. Most of all, a commitment by the leader to treat the team with respect regardless of their ambitions and celebrate team wins whenever possible.

FOUR POSSIBLE PERSONALITIES

Another consideration for a leader to consider when building a team is where a potential team member falls in the four quadrants of human capability.

Can Do and Will Do These are the team members every leader wants! They step into the team well trained and ready to take off at a run. These people are diamonds to find, but like diamonds, take some work to locate. **Can't Do but Will Do** These are team members that are ready and willing, but require some work to become effective. Another great addition to the team, but the team leader should account for the time and energy to bring this team member up to speed.

Can Do but Won't Do These folks are a challenge for team leaders to understand. The burning question is why or what is preventing this team member from contributing to the team. Team leaders are challenged to determine if there are barriers that stop the individual and attempt to mitigate those issues. These team members are not automatic throwaways, but can become a drag on the team if the leader does not address the issue quickly and fairly. **Can't Do and Won't Do** These are people best passed over in the search for new employees. This is tough to do in a high unemployment situation, but another warm body that can't and won't contribute to the team is a time waster no leader can afford.

SO YOU HAVE A TEAM, NOW WHAT?

Jack Welch, retired CEO of General Electric, once said, "It's all about people because in the end it's all people. It's picking the best people. It's motivating the best people. It's rewarding the best people in the soul and the wallet. It's hugging them. It's doing all these things to them. It's making them great. It's being excited by their success. It's all those things."

Jack knew what he was talking about back in the heyday of GE. While he was sometimes viewed as a ruthless leader, he completely understood that without the best people in the company, success would be a challenge. He understood that a successful company meant job security for his employees. Jack knew that time spent in hiring the right person for the best fit in the company would pay dividends. He understood the power of decentralized, self-managed teams. He understood that compensation had to reflect performance. Jack believed in lots of training and the creation of a "we" feeling of a team instead of the "us and them" of labor and management. And Jack understood that keeping employees in the dark benefited no one, so he built trust through sharing critical information with his teams.

TEAM ENVIRONMENT

Everything starts with people. The leader's job is to hire the best, develop their skills, and make them part of a team, encourage continuous learning, give team members responsibility for organizational outcomes, and trust in self-management. Maybe most important, it's up to the leaders at every level to reduce stress on the team caused by those outside disruptions that are always present in any organization.

If the leader can set up that type of environment for his or her people, the work they do, (the products they make and the services they deliver), should be of good quality.

CREATING LANES

Once the right people are in place the leader needs to provide the freedom to operate within certain parameters, we will call them lanes, for each of their subordinates to work between the guardrails set up. This provides employees the freedom to operate within their lane, but also establishes the circumstances when leadership must come along to assist with an unusual situation that may arise from time to time.

Creating lanes includes implementing or developing policies and operating procedures, (sometimes called standard operating procedures or SOPs), and then educating and training the employee on these parameters that the employee can safely work within. For those that work within the physical world, the SOP may establish certain frequencies that a given task is performed, certain levels of stocking materials, certain procedures to be followed for any given task, and procedures to be followed when events are observed that indicate some part of their work begins to fall outside accepted limits. For those working on a white collar team, there will still be certain procedures that would be followed to achieve success and those should be captured as well.

Policies are implemented to establish the understanding of why and how the team members are expected to conduct themselves and to set minimum levels of expectations for team and /or customer relations.

Policies may establish things such as communication etiquette: the team will respond to phone calls, emails or texts within an established time, or expectations regarding team or customer relationships.

The employee must be trained in the policies and procedures (P&P) of the organization and evaluated on their understanding of how well they understand the intent and expected outcomes set in those documents.

Good policies and procedures that establish lanes of performance and responsibility for the leader and team members should remove the burdensome management of the most routine tasks, freeing the employee to have control over their day and freeing the leader to focus on the team performance.

Once the team is in place and operating within their lanes, the leader should periodically evaluate the processes within the team to determine if there are changes that sometimes creep in and become sand in the gears of the team. We live in a rapidly changing world; new technology is always being developed, governmental regulations ebb and flow, and many other changes occur on a regular basis that may impact the team. Leaders today no longer have the luxury of the good old days when tasks did not change, orders could be given and followed, and the whistle blew at five o'clock to send people home. It is up to the leader to be aware of new tools, new regulations, to capture lessons learned by the staff in their daily encounters and to bring in the team to have input into making ethical decisions that impact the team. It is also incumbent for the leader to watch for team members that may be struggling, either as new members of the team or mature team members that may be experiencing some external or internal challenges.

OPERATING "IN CONTROL"

Once the organization is functioning "in control" (a term used by W. Edwards Deming to describe a high functioning team under his concept of Total Quality Management), the leader can then focus on the anomalies that impact team performance.

Deming described a tool for leaders called PDSA, for Plan, Do, Study and Act. Others used the PDCA cycle or Plan, Do, Check and Act. These evaluation cycles are usually applied in the strategic planning conducted at the business or department level (discussed in another chapter), but can also be used in evaluating tools, methods, and policies and procedures that are established and how well the individuals within the leaders span of control follow those procedures.

With the tool of policies and procedures in place and with buy-in from the team, the leader can then begin to look, using the PDSA cycle, for those things that may negatively impact the output of the team. The leader should look for consensus within the group regarding the task at hand, distinctiveness in individual performance, and the consistency of individual performance (Kinicki and Kreitner 2003 pg. 72-74).

The leader, after the team is trained on the policies and procedures, should first look at the degree of consensus within the group as to how well the organizations P&Ps are being followed. If there are ten team members and nine of the ten demonstrate a behavior of working within the P&Ps, then the leader should determine why the individual with the outlying behavior does not share the consensus of the group. Was the training understood, were the expectations clear, or is there some bias within the individual's culture that impacts their work? After close evaluation, the individual may require additional training and if that fails to improve performance, then a corrective action plan may need to be implemented for the individual.

The second observation the leader should make, providing the consensus of the group, regarding the P&Ps, is to the distinctiveness of individual performance. In this case, distinctiveness applies to an individual performing the prescribed number of tasks, say six distinctive tasks, where five tasks are performed within the lanes created by the P&Ps and one task is not up to standard. In other words, if a team member typically meets or exceeds expectations on most of the tasks in their work, but has less than expected results on one task, then the leader's obligation is to determine why an otherwise high performing team member is struggling in one area. The leader should meet with the team member, not necessarily to implement a corrective action plan, but rather to understand what may be the issue. It could be something as simple as re-training, an improper tool, or some outside influence. The leader may discover that a certain accommodation for a physical challenge may need to be implemented. The process may take some work to discover the problem and may require some of the problem solving skills discussed elsewhere within this book.

A high performing team that understands their responsibilities and limitations will free the leader to focus on immediate issues that do not necessarily fall within typical day to day operations that would otherwise tend to impact the effectiveness of the team.

TYPES AND FORMATION OF TEAMS

Teams or groups tend to be either formal or informal, where a formal team is created by leadership to address certain specified issues. Informal teams tend to be more relationship based and may be more of a social group.

Formal teams have a specified objective and are expected to define and solve complex issues. Teams usually form from within a standard work group and are tasked to address specified issues and in this context the team may be an additional duty outside the routine of work. These teams work on two levels, the team as a whole and the individuals that make up the team. The team may be a permanent or semi-permanent entity, but team members may come and go from time to time. The individuals on a given team have certain needs that need to be met including the need to feel like a productive member of a larger group. In addition there is the need to develop a sense of identity within the team and be able to let down their guard with other team members.

New teams that form typically go through several identified phases, forming, storming, norming, and performing.

Forming is an interesting time. The group comes together for the first time where they have a chance to get to know one another. The health-care company that I worked for used a number of tools to get teams to open up and relax with one another. There was usually a game like "two truths and a lie" where others could get a feel of who each other were. During the forming process, we would go to dinner together and allow some undefined time in a social setting to further develop relationships.

Storming is exactly what it sounds like in that team members may begin to challenge one another or leadership in an attempt to determine what the boundaries of the group may be. This is not necessarily a bad phase for the team, but it is a dangerous phase if leadership cannot guide the team through successfully to the next phase of norming. Many teams stall out in the storming phase and never become an effective team.

Norming is where the team settles down and begins to adopt a "we" mentality and the team opens up to honest and matter of fact communication, setting aside the emotional drivers that may have been present during the storming phase.

Performing teams are the objective of all of the work and effort expended to get the team to the stage where problems are solved and genuine progress is made toward a stated objective or goal.

Adjournment is the time when the specific work is done and team members move back to their daily routine or are challenged with another opportunity. This is a time to celebrate and recognize the efforts of the team for a job well done.

Some teams work together long enough that team members retire or leave the company for other reasons, so what can the leader do to ensure the original objectives are accomplished? Each new member should be oriented regarding the original purpose of the team and the desired outcomes of the team's effort. A small ceremony may be considered and at the very least, time set aside to introduce the new members and honor those that remain.

Consider having one of the team mentor the new member to provide them with the initial purpose of the team and a historical perspective of the work, including any written records of progress.

MORE ABOUT TQM AND ITS DERIVATIVES

Why is a segment about TQM included in a work on leadership? Theory Y of leadership proposes that most people do not have to be forced to perform, but will do so willingly if the conditions they work in meet certain parameters. Having been a student of TQM since a revival of sorts in the 1990s, I came to appreciate the value of Deming's work, but there is a big caution to consider if you want to go down this path.

I was President and CEO of a regional construction company with 85 employees and about $15 million in gross revenue in the early '90s as well as a 50% partner in the company. I could see waste and inefficiency draining profit off of projects and searched for a way to stop the losses and increase profitability. Our local Chamber of Commerce subscribed to a ten-episode series of a seminar broadcasted weekly to our local community college. Many businesses in town participated, and it was especially exciting since Deming was still alive and spoke in several of the segments. I was on fire with excitement and immediately went to work to make my company a TQM company. I failed miserably since I was the only one interested and could not implement this model from the top down.

The next year, there was a follow on series of ten TQM seminars and I went back to see where I went wrong. It was obvious, my first step had to be creating buy-in to the concept. Then I began with small steps which produced small wins. The effort grew and within a few years, we applied for the State Level Baldridge award and achieved level one. More importantly, profit margins began to improve as we put these new practices to work. Unfortunately, I do not believe my partner really understood what we were attempting to do and was simply going through the motions and that created a division within the company that was obvious to all, leading eventually to my departure from the company.

TQM became Six Sigma, and Six Sigma became something with a different name, but the underlying principals remained the same. My personal opinion was that some doctoral student needed something for a dissertation and tinkered with Deming's work enough to give it a new name. Just a personal opinion and I have no evidence to share on the subject.

TQM was introduced elsewhere in this work, but the topic is so powerful that it is appropriate to get into the subject in more detail. Leaders and teams committed to TQM should read more on the subject. The Deming Management Method by Mary Walton is an excellent resource for those wanting to begin a quality program.

During World War 2, the U.S. military had an overwhelming need to gain control over some very complex tasks. The United States had to build a war machine like none other before and new methods were necessary to make the unimaginable commonplace. President Roosevelt wanted various plane manufacturers to build 1,000 planes a day; while Ford did not build 1,000 planes a day, with this new method of management developed in part by Bell Labs, Ford did build a B-24 Bomber every 63 minutes at its Willow Run plant in Michigan.

Every 63 minutes a reliable, capable, and imposing B-24 was completed.

Bell Labs, part of Bell Telephone, began to study the need to be able to develop reliable products in a limited amount of time in 1920. Total Quality Management was first used in Bell Labs and the concept began to be fleshed out with control measures that would contribute to a process with fewer or virtually no defects. These were some of the tools employed by Ford at Willow Run and those processes worked.

The war machine was successful, first with Germany and several of its allies surrendering and then a few months later, Japan capitulated in an unconditional surrender. General MacArthur was tasked with the creation of a new constitution for the Japanese people and restoration of a completely devastated economy. There were almost no manufacturing capabilities left, and the US recognized that it was in the best interest of the world economy if order and opportunity were restored in Japan.

Interestingly, possibly due in large part to the US dominating the world with manufacturing capability after the war, the employment of TQM began to wane. At the same time, W.E. Deming was tasked with helping rebuild the Japanese economy. Deming took the tools developed at the Bell Labs and employed so well during the war, and landed, briefcase in hand, in a devastated Japan.

Deming began to work with the government and business leaders to implement TQM and the Japanese embraced the efforts. The success of that work is still visible on the streets of the United States today with the Honda Accord, the most common car in the US, making up 3% of vehicles on the road in 2020. Toyota and Honda make up six of the top ten cars sold during that same period. Quality of these vehicles surpassed many domestic brands.

TQM began to resurface in the US as a management philosophy in the 1970s. There were different brands like GE's Six Sigma, Baldridge, and others, but the concepts were generally similar, and in this discussion we will use TQM to represent the various, but similar philosophies. For a period of time, business once again focused on the Total Quality Management concept, but in the 2020s the concept seems to have once ceased to be top of mind.

PRINCIPLES OF TQM

The basic principles of TQM are focused on the continual achievement of high customer satisfaction achieved by a systems approach using proper tools, techniques and training. The principals require a commitment to continuous improvement in order to maintain high customer satisfaction in an ever changing environment.

Regardless of the name associated with a quality improvement program and the scope of the program, there are four common principals:

Do things right the first time

Listen to and learn from customers and employees.

Make continuous improvement part of the team DNA that is acknowledged every day.

Build teamwork, trust and mutual respect.

TQM is, to a large extent, employee driven, which implies that every employee be committed to continuous learning and a willing participant in the effort to achieve the best customer satisfaction.

The interesting thing to note about the principals of TQM is there is no mention of profit or cost reduction. The underlying message is that a company or team that focuses on satisfying the customer will be the preferred team, vendor, or supplier which builds a loyal customer base. Why would anyone prefer an inferior product or service, even at a lower price? Of course there are limits to the price point at which a decision may be made to save up front cost, but an astute customer will consider initial cost only as a part of the cost equation with the understanding that operational cost may go up for an inferior product.

The second consideration that should ultimately affect profitability is the efficiency that becomes imbedded in the processes of an organization committed to Total Quality Management.

Simply put, a focus on profit may or not yield the desired result, while high customer satisfaction and loyalty along with lower operating cost resulting from the efficiencies of TQM should result in profit, or lowered cost of operations.

DEMING'S FOCUS ON PEOPLE

When Deming spoke about TQM, he chose to focus on the management aspect of the TQM equation. Similar to the focus on process and customer satisfaction ultimately yielding profit, Deming focused on management knowing that managers using the principals of "good management" would yield quality.

Deming's focus on people (employees/team members) calls for the following:

Formal training in statistical process control techniques and teamwork

Helpful leadership or a coach rather focusing on giving orders and punishing nonperformance.

Elimination of fear so employees are not reluctant to ask questions or challenge the status quo.

Focus on continuous process improvements rather than a numerical quota.

Elimination of barriers to good workmanship.

The above five points are distilled from Deming's fourteen points of Management and seven Deadly Diseases of Management and are useful when considering entering the Total Quality journey. Those wanting to drill down further have a number of resources available that can assist the reader in developing a TQM program that fits the expertise and resources available.

TRAINING

Continuous learning has been mentioned before, but deserves drilling down to understand what continuous learning is and is not.

Virtually every team has a knowledge base that must be an integral part of their employment. This knowledge base may be focused on business specific topics that are a requirement to initial employment and then annually thereafter for continued employment. The requirements may include specific safety training, emergency management training, and training on expected rules or codes of conduct in the organization, certification or re-certification training specific to the particular job.

Formal training on statistical process is over and above the standard initial and annual refresh for the basic requirements of the organization. Training on statistical process and teamwork may sound intimidating, but at its most basic level, the employee is trained on identifying problems and how to analyze those problems that may impact the team and their product. We will discuss specific problem solving tools later. This training is not intended to make everyone on the team a statistician with a degree in statistical analysis, but rather to develop an ability to recognize the sand in the gears of the operation and propose solution.

PROBLEM SOLVING TOOLS

Ask why five times. This one is really simple and is designed to drill down to the most basic issue in a problem. It can also drive people nuts if they do not understand this is simply a way to peel the layers of a failure away just like removing the skin of an onion, but it reduces the opportunity for spending time and effort to fix a symptom of a problem rather than the cause of a problem.

An example could be showing up late for work with the first question, "Why were you late for work?" Let's say the answer is "I ran out of gas." So the question is "Why did you run out of gas?" The answer is "I didn't have time to stop at the gas station this morning." "Why didn't you have time to stop at the gas station this morning?" "My alarm did not go off on time." "Why did your alarm not work?" And so on until the basic problem is uncovered in the late to work saga.

In the "late to work example", the root cause may have been a failure to update the clock time for daylight savings time, so the solution is not gas for the car, or a new alarm clock, but rather a reminder to set the clock back.

The example is simplistic, but hopefully provides an example the use of this particular tool.

The fishbone diagram. The fishbone or Ishikawa diagram is a method developed by Kaoru Ishikawa, a key figure in the development of quality initiatives in Japan. Ishikawa integrated and expanded the management theories of Deming and developed additional tools to use in the process.

The fishbone diagram is a good tool to visualize and guide team discussion when considering the basic, or root, cause of a process problem. The diagram designed to capture the various inputs to a problem, and usually incorporates asking why five times as the diagram is filled out. A completed diagram provides a way to drill down into the potential root causes of a problem.

Elements of a fishbone diagram can vary depending on the particular circumstances of the team, but one common example focuses on **People, Policies, Procedures, and Equipment,** and occasionally two more elements of money and maintenance are incorporated.

Five benefits of a Fishbone Diagram are: logical display of inputs, all contributing inputs are displayed simultaneously, provides a roadmap for brainstorming, helps the team drill down to the root cause(s), and help the team focus on the problem.

Using the Fishbone diagram is a very dynamic process and best described in the YouTube videos associated with this book.

COACHING

Every spring and summer, professional baseball teams take to the field. Some have a few team members with extraordinary talent, but most players are very good at what they do and have developed that skill from little league through Division 1 sports. Those teams that play in October have another winning talent and that is the manager that can recognize how to deploy talent, understand when coaching is required to bring a player back to peak performance, sense when fatigue or personal problems are affecting player performance, and generally keep a finger on the pulse of the players on the field or on the bench at any given time.

How hard can that be?

Out of 400 million or so North Americans (US, Canada, and Mexico), there are thirty Major League managers and 840 players at any given time. These managers and players are the cream of the crop; the best at what they do. But only two teams play at the end of October.

Few teams can claim the talent of a major league team, but the concepts of developing and management are the same. The winning coach sifts through potential talent, understands who should and should not end up on the team, and works to keep that team functioning at the highest level possible.

Deming was astute and recognized that coaches were much more desirable than dictatorial leadership with commands and punishment.

THE FEAR FREE ENVIRONMENT

Removing fear from the leader/team member environment is more art than science. Leaders have inherent power over others; the power to hire and fire, the power to influence raises, the power to assign the plum jobs and the power to generally make life miserable. It is important the leader be self-aware and careful in the exercise of that power.

Conversely, team members have a significant amount of power; power to make discrimination or wrongful discharge claims, power to report actual or perceived injustice to upper management, and the power to influence their peers. Employees in a union environment have an even greater advantage in the strength of the union to intervene to address perceived or actual wrongs. **Note to leaders: Know your state and local labor laws, and in a union environment, understand the union agreements as they relate to your team.**

Discipline and documentation are addressed otherwise in this writing, but the main takeaway for the leader is concept of fairness. If people believe they are treated fairly, they typically respond positively. Another way to consider fairness is application of the Golder Rule and that is simply treating others the way you would like to be treated in the same circumstances.

So how does a leader remove fear from the working environment without diminishing their ability to lead? Fairness, of course, combined with firmness, or the velvet glove of leadership.

Discipline in a fear free environment. Almost all jobs have rules that must be met like showing up on time without distractions or certain expectations of dress or sobriety that the work requires. There are also certain expectations of performance and productivity that must be met. The first time the leader allows substandard performance, the team quickly perceives an injustice and team performance will suffer. While disciplining a team member may seem incongruent with the need to drive out fear, discipline is key to a high performing team.

Think for a moment about high performing military teams. High standards are set by leaders and under performers are quickly evaluated for additional training or the less desirable option of removing a member from the team. If the members believe that everyone on the team is functioning at a high level of performance, pride in being part of the organization grows and willingness to support one another and their leader grows. The work may be unpleasant, to say the least, and the team may suffer from all sorts of discomfort, but they are willing to do so because they are treated fairly and meeting high expectations. The breakdown in team performance is rapid and hard to repair if a leader turns a blind eye to poor performance.

High expectations and discipline do not introduce fear into the team environment, unless it is the concern of the individual that they may not live up to the expectations of their peers.

An Open Door Policy. Team leader's calendars may be packed full with meetings, calls, planning sessions and dozens of other emergent issues, so a leader must be intentional with setting aside a time when team members can come in without an appointment to speak about issues of concern.

Sometimes the issues regard team performance or personnel conflicts that may arise from time to time. Other open door visits may also concern a personal issue that a team member is dealing with. Regardless of the nature of the open door visit, it is incumbent upon leadership to keep confidences shared by the team member. In some circumstances there is nothing to be done but to listen, and that may be enough. In no circumstances should the leader dismiss the team members' concern. There are times when an open door visit is an indicator of a hidden problem and leaders should ask the questions, sometimes five times, to get to the real issue of concern.

Boundaries on personal relationships. Team leaders have to be aware of personal attacks, both from team members, and sometimes even from themselves. Team members need to know that there can be impassioned speech about a policy, procedure, vendor, or some other issue internal or external to the team, but personal attacks are not allowed.

The team environment should be such that people are comfortable to speak without being shouted down or disparaged by other team members.

Praise in public, discipline in private. This is discussed in other sections of this work, but this is important enough to say again. This shows respect for team members and respect from leaders and peers is a building block for a fear free environment.

FOCUS ON CONTINUOUS PROCESS IMPROVEMENTS RATHER THAN A NUMERICAL QUOTA.

This seems counterintuitive at first glance. How does on improve without measuring somehow the delta between what things used to be and some desired future state. The need to count and measure does not go away with the application of TQM, but how those numbers are used does change.

The question in a non-TQM environment is typically "How many widgets did you make in a certain time period?" In a TQM environment, that question changes into something like, "Is there something in our process that, if changed, would allow us to make more widgets or reduce the number of defective widgets?" In the second example, the numbers become a measurement of an improved process rather than an arbitrary quota.

Deming's red bead experiment. In Deming's seminars, there was an audience participation activity that demonstrated the focus on process rather than quotas. There would be a certain number of beads, red and white in color. For this example, the red beads and white beads were mixed together in a bin. Participants were selected from the audience and each given a paddle with a number of holes and each participant was to dip the paddle with the objective of getting no more than 5 red beads out of the 50 beads captured in a given cycle. The number of the red beads varied wildly, and only a few times were five or less red beads captured on the paddle, with most of the time there were many more than five captured.

Deming would dismiss audience members that exceeded the five bead quota until all of the participants were gone and the red bead company was out of business.

The point of the demonstration was that all of the participants were willing and desired to make the arbitrary five bead quota, but the process and equipment simply would not allow for anything other than random success.

The reader can Google "Deming's red bead experiment" and see an actual demonstration.

WILLING WORKERS AND BROKEN PROCESSES

Generally speaking, most team members want to do a good job and contribute to the team, but they have to work within the constraints of the system. Talented, willing workers encountering a broken system that impacts performance typically will do one of several things; work to correct the system, leave for a better environment, or decide to stay in a mediocre environment.

The first instance when team members want to help improve the system, which then is combined with a team leader that understand the tools and benefits of team participation is the sweet spot that yields a high performing team.

The second instance where talented people have no ownership in decision making and choose to leave creates a revolving door where the team leader's time is consumed in constantly bringing new people on staff.

The third instance is a death knell for the team. The organization is left with mediocre performers that have no ownership in the team except for the paycheck on Friday.

ELIMINATE BARRIERS TO GOOD WORKMANSHIP

Possibly the most important task for a team leader is to vigilantly look for the "sand in the gears" that can wear down team members as surely as the grit of sand will bring a machine to a halt.

The opportunity to build new process from the ground up does not present very often: typically initial processes are modified over time as new policies are developed, new materials are introduced, and new governmental regulations are introduced or for any number of other reasons. If there is not a thorough review of the changed process, some superfluous requirements can remain.

Annual reviews of policy and procedure manuals by the team leader and those in the team that are directly affected. Reviews may be required sooner if there is a sudden change to anyone of the inputs in a process.

STRATEGIC PLANNING

In another chapter, I referenced the belief that Winston Churchill actually is credited with saying "He who fails to plan is planning to fail." Of course Helmuth von Moltke, Chief of Staff for the Prussian Army in 1871, said, "No plan survives contact with the enemy." So where does the truth lie between these two quotes? As odd as it seems, they were both correct.

Churchill was correct that without a plan, the result is a kind of "no matter where you go, there you are" type of a mentality; a life where if you consistently miss the target with your arrow, simply move the target for better results.

Moltke was correct, but he did not speak to the benefits of how a good plan can expose alternative realities and potential response. In other words, it is easier and more efficient to shift a good plan as needed than to simply blunder around with no plan at all and relinquish any control over your own destiny.

These are military examples, but they are relevant to any organization or team. In the civilian world, the plan is typically a strategic plan that is the result of much effort to attempt to discern the future state of the organization as it operates within the larger future environment. Any time the future is considered, it is our human effort to see ahead a year, five years, or more. Not everything in the plan may come to pass, but in a well-made and well thought out plan, enough of the plan will materialize to make the effort worthwhile.

Strategic planning is a discipline learned in business and management degree programs or certifications, or may be self-taught by reading the literature regarding the topic. Whenever possible, it is desirable to have an independent third-party guide the planning process to keep the discussion in the center of the new proposed road as much as possible. Those trained in facilitating strategic planning will usually move the process along efficiently with less rework on the behalf of the participants.

Subordinate leaders may think they do not have a contribution to make in a strategic plan, but that is not so and will be discussed in the development of tactics. It is not practical to engage the entire organization in strategic planning unless the organization is very small, so most of the time representatives from various disciplines within an organization will be selected to participate in the process. The planning group can become unwieldy if it becomes too large and the ideal number of participants, at least in my experience, is ten to twelve, as long as that represents a slice of the organization.

Strategic planning is a structured process that guides the participants and promotes free thinking. The facilitator's obligation is to keep the discussion on track and to capture the thought developed in the process. Ultimately the facilitator will draft the initial plan for the teams review and publish the final product. In some instances, the facilitator will be retained to assist with subordinate teams as they develop the supporting structure for the plan.

Generally speaking, the planning group tasked to develop a new or updated strategic plan should include key leaders and stakeholders and department heads that will be impacted by the results of any plan. The caution is to keep the planning group to a manageable size, preferably no more than twelve to fifteen individuals. Ground rules must be set and enforced to avoid off topic discussions and to avoid personal attacks. Attempts to solve second and third level downstream problems as they are identified should be avoided.

Anticipate at least two partial or full days for small organizations for the initial planning process. Larger organizations' planning sessions may extend over a longer period of time. Once the group addresses the elements (listed below), the information should be captured in a standard format and returned to the full planning group for review. The final goals and objectives should be shared with the appropriate parties within the organization to allow development of objectives and tactics for all the various departments or elements of the organization. This is where leaders at every level, along with as many of their team as is feasible, determine the tactics used for a specific part of the organization. Developing these tactics may require some extended time to complete.

Once the departmental objectives and tactics are developed and that work "scored" as to budgetary and personnel impact, then those are presented for consideration for inclusion in the overall plan. This model anticipates a rather large organization and smaller organizations may be able to accomplish this work in a reduced time.

As a structured process there are certain elements that should be incorporated into the plan and the descriptions of the elements have a certain meaning that all should clearly understand.

THE STRATEGIC PLAN

The elements of a strategic plan are:

- **Mission Statement**
- **SWOT Analysis**
- **Goals**
- **Objectives**
- **Strategies or tactics**
- **Specific plans for various elements of the organization, (may be required in larger organizations)**
- **Feedback mechanism**

The Mission Statement is a broadly stated and durable statement of an organizations purpose or intent. The mission statement should address subjects including:

- Why does the organization exist?
- What is the organizations economic goals?
- What is the organizations operating philosophy regarding quality of service, the desired image of the organization, and what the organization (people) believes itself to be?
- What are we good at and what competitive advantage do we have?
- Who are our customers and how well do we understand them?
- What do we understand our responsibilities to be to the owners, our employees, and the community or world we work in?
- How well do we understand our competition?

Mission statements tend to remain fixed for extended periods of time, often many years, but should be reviewed whenever the strategic planning process is undertaken to ensure that a seismic shift has not occurred that would change the stated mission.

The SWOT Analysis is a two-part analysis, one which is an internal look at the **strengths** and **weaknesses** of the organization and the second is an evaluation of external **opportunities** and **threats** that apply to the organization. An efficient method for this activity is using Post-it notes where every participant writes their thoughts which are then placed under the appropriate SWOT category.

Once this exercise concludes, an attempt should be made to eliminate duplicates and to group the comments as best as possible in order to move into the next step of developing organizational goals. Problem solving tools may be used at this stage of the plan to drill down to the basic issues that need to be addressed.

Goals are the next step in the process. Goals are precise and measurable, address specific critical issues, should be challenging but achievable, and have specific time allotted for achievement.

While a Mission statement may be a broad brush overview of an organization, Goals are much more specific and must include measurable activities and will state who will accomplish what by when. No organization has unlimited resources and the outcome of the SWOT analysis provides a tool to identify those things which are within the organizations budget and personnel to accomplish.

Objectives, much like overall goals as described above, may be necessary to further break a Goal into work that is specific to a department of the larger organization. Goals may cover all the departments in an organization, while Objectives may be more specific to a smaller group.

Strategies or tactics specify the "who, what when, where, how and why" and are designed to support the overall goals or objectives of the organization. If the goal or objective requires completion by a certain date, then the tactics to achieve that goal need to fit together within that set time frame. Developing strategies and tactics is best left to the leader and their team that encounter the issues that are to be addressed on a regular basis. Problem solving tools are once again deployed to assure the tactic is actually addressing the basic issue rather than the symptoms of the problematic issue. An earlier discussion regarding planning and organizing recommended breaking large tasks into very specific elements and then stringing them together using a tool like Microsoft Project.

Feedback mechanisms need to be identified and reported out on regularly at a period set by the planning group. The feedback is used to determine the performance of the Strategic Plan and may indicate the plan is on track or that elements of the plan should be re-evaluated to determine if it is still relevant.

Remember, the intent of this section on Strategic Planning is for familiarization only. Local resources like Universities or Community Colleges may have personnel trained to facilitate Strategic Planning. In addition, having an independent facilitator may work to keep bias out of the finished plan.

Strategic Plans are not a "once and done" document that goes on the shelf until the next planning session. Leaders at all levels must hold themselves and their staff accountable to achieve the plans goals, objectives and tactics or the plan will be a "busted plan" and a waste of organization resources.

ETHICS AND LEADERSHIP

Team Leadership has potential for great rewards, and it also has the opportunity for things to not go so well from time to time. There may be times when leaders do everything "right", but it may not seem to matter. The potential for criticism exists in every organization so how best to position oneself for that moment? One answer is ethical leadership.

Other parts of this document refer to the Golden Rule of treating others the way you would like to be treated, but there may be difficult times when team leaders need to make unpleasant choices that affect their team members. Choices that have results leaders themselves would not like to be on the receiving end of must sometimes be made, so how does a leader justify delivering bad news to a team member that they themselves would not like to receive? There is no magic answer, except to build the character required for the job.

The ethical challenge. There are a number of ethical theories that could be considered, and it is difficult to fault the choice of a certain ethical foundation that underlies the way a leader lives their life. The problem comes when a leader is not *consistent* in their application of ethical leadership.

A leader's ethical foundation is a product of many things: religion, family, community, and more all contribute to the "ethics" of a leader and most people do not even think about how all of these contributions add up to an ethical way of life. So how does a leader formalize that foundation so that it stands when the winds come and the water rises?

All of the major world religions have approaches to ethical decisions that can be similar in some circumstances and very different in others. It is very likely that today's leaders will have members on their teams from a variety of backgrounds, religions, no religion, cultures, races, genders and more. Leaders cannot be everything to everyone; that squishy approach does no one any favors and will ultimately have a negative impact on those on the leader's team. At the same time, leaders should develop an appreciation of ethical considerations that others may have that are different from the leaders.

Note the use of the word appreciation. This implies that a leader may understand a different ethical approach, but not necessarily approve of a particular application of ethics. Leaders first must understand their own ethical foundation, then the ethical position of the organization; if those two ethical approaches do not align, then the leader should decide if this is the right organization to be a part of. In regard to team members, as long as their beliefs do not violate organizational precepts, are not illegal, and are not disruptive to the team, the leader should work to accommodate different viewpoints without judgment.

An ethical choice. The Golden Rule, treat others like you would like to be treated, is a great building block for an ethical foundation. There are other ethical theories that could be considered, but for ethics in business, an ethical theory called <u>utilitarianism</u> may be the most implemented. Utilitarianism, at its most basic, determines right from wrong based on the outcomes of a decision. Simply stated, utilitarianism ethics holds that the most ethical choice is the one that will produce the greatest good for the greatest number. The reader is encouraged to read and learn from themselves more about other ethical viewpoints they may adopt.

An example of utilitarian ethics may be a situation where budget requirements may require a choice between a reduction in force and the potential demise of the company. In this particular example, terminating an employee is certainly not treating someone the way you would want to be treated. The leader can, however, be compassionate, caring, and work to make the transition as easy as possible.

The fact is that anyone aspiring to be a leader will eventually have to deliver bad news. News that may have a ripple effect through families and friends. The leader that does not understand what makes up their ethical foundation or who is inconsistent in their relationship with others will not be in a solid position to act when action is required.

CORPORATE AND TEAM CULTURE—ARE WE REALLY WHO WE SAY WE ARE?[1]

While ethics is a personal trait, culture would apply to the organization writ large.

The dictionary definition of culture can include an appreciation of the arts, but in the context of a team or organization, the meaning of the word has to do with the customs, traditions, heritage, habits and so on, of the team or company (Kinicki and Kreitner 2003 pg. 24-30). Common to the military is the term "esprit de corps", which is defined as a feeling of pride, fellowship, and common loyalty shared by members of a particular group.

All teams have a culture; it may be a culture of high performance or a culture of punishing those that perform above the norm of the group, but good or poor, it is still the culture.

In the study of organizational behavior, three elements of culture have been identified: observable artifacts or what others see, espoused written or spoken values identified as important to the team, and expressed or enacted values that are exhibited by the team.

Observable artifacts or what others see. I once visited the office of a general contractor in Ft. Collins, Colorado. The workspace in the office was open and right in the middle of that space was a fairly large brass bell about 16 inches in overall height. During the course of the conversation, the subject of the bell came up and the owner of the business said that whenever the company won a low bid on a project or when a new contract was negotiated, the person that had the most responsibility for the win, would ring the bell. Work would stop for a few moments and all those in the office would applaud the person or team that won the privilege to ring the bell.

People were hungry to ring that bell. The sound of it spurred everyone around to work harder just for the chance to be the one, the favored one that rang the bell. No matter that after a few minutes of celebration, it was all business as they moved on to getting the next job, but there was a shiny brass moment that was shared.

Artifacts are the visible part of the culture that people see when they walk in the door. Do all wear a company Polo shirt? Do all use the same words and tell the same stories? Surprisingly, artifacts can be changed easier than some of the embedded actions that may not be as visible.

Espoused Values or what others hear us say. Values usually have five key elements; stated beliefs, an identified end state, true regardless of circumstances, a guide for behaviors the team sees as important and the measuring stick for actual behavior, and values are usually ranked in importance.

Nothing better for a mid-day break on a hot day than an ice cold cola and the folks at Coca-Cola hope that it is a Coke you have in that frosty glass. Coca-Cola may be a drink that is largely unchanged for over a hundred years (with the possible exception of the New Coke debacle back in the last century), that has seven values that are the espoused values that are out in public for all to see:

- Leadership: The courage to shape a better future
- Collaboration: Leverage collective genius
- Integrity: Be real
- Accountability: If it is to be, it's up to me
- Passion: Committed in heart and mind

- Diversity: As inclusive as our brands
- Quality: What we do, we do well

McDonald's would love to sell you that Coke along with a burger and fries, maybe even supersized. I have been fortunate to have traveled a fair amount having been in every state in the US and in more than 20 countries and after enjoying the local restaurants for a few days or weeks, a good old American McDonald's quarter pounder with cheese, fries with ketchup and a frosty Coke begins to weigh heavily on my mind. And they always taste the same whether I'm in the south of Spain or Dodge City, Kansas.

Their company values are:

- Serve: We put our customers and people first
- Inclusion: We open our doors to everyone
- Integrity: We do the right thing
- Community: We are good neighbors
- Family: We get better together

Expressed or enacted values. These are the things teams and organizations do that may or may not line up with the fancy shirts and high sounding values. Generally speaking, the Quarter Pounders, Big Macs, fries and that frosty Coke almost always taste the same. The restrooms are usually clean and up to date, and the service generally friendly and fast. Until it's not.

There are over 38,000 McDonalds in over 100 countries around the world. Most provide the same level of quality, service, and cleanliness. Occasionally there is a clinker that customers really don't want to return too. In the big scheme of things with that many locations, the clinkers are usually the exception, and the stated values generally line up with how the restaurant is run.

In those locations or in other organizations where lived values are not the same as the stated values, it really doesn't take long to notice from the outward appearance of the facility and the attitude of the employees. It is the same within a team; the team members quickly learn if the team walks the talk, and when there is a disconnect, the desired culture becomes something else, a different culture. Because there is always a culture whether planned or left to develop on its own. Always.

Remember I said observable artifacts may be easier to change than the expressed or embedded values that are not written down, but passed around by the team members with the same, or possibly greater impact on the product delivered by the team.

Creating a team or organizational culture is one of the most important things a leader can do. Changing an underlying embedded culture can be one of the hardest things a leader can attempt.

The first and most important step is for the leader to make certain their own conduct is in alignment with the observable artifacts and stated values of the organization of the team.

Next, figure out ways that the team can be shifted to the observable and stated values. This can be something as simple as ringing the metaphorical bell when a desirable action occurs, or providing a small reward for getting caught doing the right thing.

Finally, determine if there is someone that refuses to adopt the team values and remove them from the team. Remember a little yeast will act on the entire loaf of bread. If team members see the leader ignore disciplining a non-conforming member, then the entire team may begin to create their own culture. Leaders cannot tolerate disrespecting the desired culture even from the most talented person or the boss's nephew or niece.

This is where ethics and integrity matter.

WHY DOES A CULTURE MATTER?

Once, years ago, I was a Field Artillery Firing Battery Commander, a newly minted Captain with shiny Captain's insignia. It really felt good, that is until my boss, the Battalion Commander, took me aside to talk about the benefits and pitfalls of command.

I will never forget the story he related to me about how a new leader was asked by his boss to place his hand in a bucket of water and then remove it. My boss asked me, "How big a hole did you leave in the water?" It was a good object lesson on my own importance and how there were others lined up to take my place if necessary.

Teams and organizations always change; people come and go, they are promoted or fired, or even the ones that are there for life will eventually retire. So how does a team, company, or organization survive? Without the driver of an underlying culture, it usually doesn't.

Team or organizational culture exists for four distinct purposes: create an identity, align collective commitment, create stability for the organization, and finally to help team members make sense of who they are and where they fit in the larger organization.[1]

Create an organizational identity. Big Macs are the same around the world, Coca-Cola has a glass bottle that is recognizable by feel in the darkest night without a moon, 3-M sticky notes stick to the edge of computer screens all around the world; all of these companies have created a distinct organization identity. 3-M culture focuses on innovation and performance goals often included a goal to produce and sell something that had not even been invented yet. 3-M reinforced this innovative identity by awarding a specially designed trophy of a winged golden foot called the Golden Step Trophy. This trophy was awarded employees whose innovations had become a saleable product and met the company's goal.

Facilitate a collective commitment. Remember the bell in the contractor's office? The team members went to work every week with the desire to ring that bell. 3-M employees were envious of the winged foot that sat in a position of prominence and the ones that didn't have one yet, wanted one with all their being.

3-M has slightly south of 100,000 employees in 2020, and at one time had almost 44,000 employees with 15 years or more tenure.

Needless to say, turnover is fairly low and is an indicator of the commitment of the employees to the organization and this commitment plays pout in the success of the organization.

Good culture creates stability for the team members. A strong, positive culture creates a "comfort zone" for employees to work within. Even strong companies suffer downturns from time to time and how they deal with those downturns is critical to the confidence of the employees that the company or team has their interest at heart.

I worked for a Fortune 50 company that went through a down turn. The edict to reduce staff came down to my department. We were able to craft a plan to reduce staff primarily through normal attrition, inter-company transfers, and retirements, but even with that strategy, there were a few positions that would go away that were still filled. The company had an employee agreement that would allow employees terminated due to a reduction in force, with a paid period of time to allow for a new job search. The paid terminal leave was graduated based on the position the employee held within the company, based on the higher the specialization or more advanced the position, and the longer it may take to find a similar job.

The reduction in force was not a surprise, but for the most part, the team members felt they were treated with compassion, and fairness. Those that remained knew if another round of reduction were in the future, they would be treated fairly, and most of those that left, would have returned if they could.

Company culture helps the individual find and understand their fit within the organization. My daughter left a job sector with a broken culture that seemed to neither care about their people or the product they delivered. She did this without a job waiting for her and worked to make a complete pivot away from her chosen field. It's a tough way to find a job.

Finally, after a grueling job search of several months, she found a good fit. There was an initial interview, followed by interviews with the recruiter, other team members, and finally the CEO and owner of the company with an offer a week or so later. The entire process took over two months. Within a week of the offer, she received a package of company "swag"—special coffee, branded products, and other things to remind her of the great team she was joining.

During the on-boarding process, the routine stuff was discussed, but more importantly stories about the company were told, legends were shared and her place on the team was defined. It was done right.

Good company culture is welcoming and helps new hires find their way rapidly into the team, and team members with a feeling of belonging rapidly begin contributing to team goals.

So far we have considered developing a "good" culture, but not all cultures are good; my daughter experienced a non-caring, throw-away culture and it burned her out.

There are a number of identified company (team) cultures that have been identified, many of which are positive environments and some that are not. Some seem to have the same focus, but have subtle differences. The list is not all inclusive and some cultures actually display more than one of the various cultures listed.

Here are just a few examples of positive cultures:

Culture that recognizes achievement and rewards team members for setting and reaching stretch goals. Think about the brass bell in the contractor's office.

Culture that rewards creativity and encourages team members to find pleasure in their rolls and encourage development of new opportunities. Think about the earlier example of 3-M.

Cultures that focus on the human side and encourage group participation and development of interpersonal relationships. Think about companies or teams that have weekly or monthly meals catered in to build facilitate relationship building.

Below are a few examples of less desirable cultures:

- Cultures that "go along" and avoid conflict and where success is judged by the approval of others.

- Cultures that are bureaucratic and that expect conformity. The caution here is there is almost always a bureaucratic underpinning of teams and organizations expressed primarily in company or team policies and procedures. The policies can be liberating where they are used to establish methods to deal with routine events, but in some organizations the policies and procedures may become oppressive and limit personal innovation.
- Cultures that have a high degree of centralized control where team member do only what they are told and require direction from above.
- Cultures that do not reward but are quick to punish causing blame shifting and avoidance of apparent risk situations.
- Cultures that reward negative reinforcement where critical comments of others give a team member a win over a peer.
- Cultures that concentrate on positions of leadership and how well each leader controls their respective team members.
- Cultures with a win-lose reward system where leaders are encouraged to see their wins as conquests over their peers.
- Cultures that do not tolerate mistakes and demand perfection.
- Cultures where no particular culture is identifiable.

As you consider the list, which company would you like to work for or which team would you like to join?

Consider where you, as a leader, fit in the organization and the existing culture. Does the actual culture fit up with what the stated culture is? Can you morally and ethically operate within the culture, and if so, can you adapt to the culture without compromising your core values?

Organizations that understand and value their own culture will socialize and integrate new hires into the organization. Socialization usually includes an organization orientation where the basic parameters of team life are discussed and the stories (artifacts) told about the company. Orientation is sometimes followed by mentoring or shadowing for a period of time. Finally the new hire can function autonomously with an occasional tune up from their boss or mentor for those unusual events that arise from time to time.

1

2

COMMUNICATE WELL, OR NOTHING ELSE MATTERS

Leaders can have the best ideas ever, unencumbered resources, a willing team and an understanding boss, but that means nothing if you cannot communicate ideas to others. Conversely, communicating well but carelessly can be worse.

It is important to remember that taking communications for granted may be very dangerous. Consider that a leader or sender of a given communication must first translate or encode their idea into some medium (paper, email, text, face to face, zoom, etc.) then send or deliver that communication to the intended party where the message is decoded or translated based on the receiver's education, experience, bias, and any number of other factors. What could possibly go wrong?

In addition, distortion in the message may be introduced by the tendency to self-edit more unfavorable information out of a message to a senior leader or for subordinates to filter out information that may be damaging to their welfare. If the leaders or their subordinates have aspirations to move up in the organization, then communications tend to orbit around information that aids their cause. Finally, if there is a lack of trust between a leader and their subordinates or between the leader and a senior leader, distortion increases when critical information is intentionally withheld.

I am personally aware of several very smart and technically talented leaders that were careless with communications and it cost them dearly with the end of a long career with a good company. One individual liked off color humor and would share those "jokes" with a select few in his orbit until one day, he inadvertently selected the wrong email list and sent the email to all the leadership in the company. He was escorted out of the building with only a box of personal items in his possession within a few hours. It is just not worth the cost to communicate without deliberation and thought.

PERCEPTION   REALITY

Leaders should always consider how they are perceived regardless of the communication methods. Consider three different communications styles: assertive, aggressive, and non-aggressive or passive.

Assertive communication styles may push hard on a particular message, but does not attack others and allows other parties to influence the outcome of a particular issue. Direct and unambiguous language is used. Nonverbal communication is assertive, but not aggressive, with good eye contact, strong voice, appropriate facial expressions and pauses to verify the message is appropriately received. Assertive communication styles are generally appreciated and almost always preferable to the alternative communication styles.

Aggressive communication styles tend to reduce others stature in order to build the position of the message sender. Off color words may be employed, threats delivered, and judgment of others perceived behaviors is common. Nonverbal behavior may include glaring eye contact, being too physically close to others, threatening gestures, loud voice and frequently interrupting others.

Non-assertive communication styles tend to defer to others, even at the potential expense to the message sender. Squishy words are used including, "maybe, kind of" or other language that causes others to doubt the sender's message. Nonverbal behavior may include poor eye contact, poor posture, fidgeting, or a soft uncertain voice.

Another issue leaders must consider is their audience, regardless of the format used to deliver the message. Consider three common listening styles: results type personality, reasons type personality, and process type listener.

Results type personalities tend to be bottom line oriented, and want to quickly understand the results of the message they are receiving. Placing the result, or "what", at the very beginning of any communication is best. Those delivering messages to this type of personality may perceive the individual as blunt or rude.

Reasons type personalities are more interested in the rationale behind a given message. Reasons type message receivers appreciate knowing the "why", and expect to have the story of the message to be logical and delivered so they may consider each part of the message as it is delivered.

Process type personalities may be more interested in the "how" and in this case the how may include how the message affects relationships and others in the organization. They may also want to receive information peripheral to the main topic so they can to assist in their evaluation of how those relationships are impacted, and in most cases want to discuss the message in great detail. Process type personalities sometimes use indirect language which the message sender must decode in order to ensure the message is received correctly.

Finally, men and women tend to process information differently. This is not an absolute statement, but is in large part true. Men may tend to be more assertive, which may be interpreted as aggressive behavior, and tend to hide emotions and may come off as a "me" personality. Women may tend to more easily share credit for successes, ask more clarifying questions, and temper any criticism with praise.

Male-female communication is made even more challenging with the addition of different cultural backgrounds and the rise of the potential for persons to identify as some other gender than the one assigned at birth. A very good resource is a small book, *Do's and Taboos Around the World* by Roger E. Axtell along with several other books he authored on similar topics. When everything is considered, appropriate communication may be the most challenging issue for leaders today.

The lost art of writing effective letters. Way back in the last century, people would actually take a pen in hand (or sit down to a typewriter) and compose a letter. There were standard formats for every type of correspondence and specific instructions on how to create an address or signature block. People were actually taught how to set margins and there was often only one font on the typewriter they were using.

We have moved on well beyond using erasers and White Out (or maybe called liquid paper which was used to correct a typing error), and that is a good thing. Maybe.

Leaders are judged by their communication skills, writing in this instance, but those skills may not be in the curriculum or only referenced briefly. An excellent book for your bookshelf is *The Art of Writing Effective Letters* by Fruehling and Bouchard published way back in 1972, which is still available to order online as of 2022. This book has stood the test of time and, when referenced for correspondence, could set your letter or email in a class of its own which just may be enough to get that valuable second look.

In any event, a well written letter is very classy and should gain attention, particularly given that most of your peers may not even think of using anything other than a text.

Email. Most email communication is routine but from time to time there are sensitive issues that require written correspondence. Most sensitive matters are best discussed face to face (or at the very least on a phone call, but more about that later). The most important thing to remember about email is that *it can last forever.* You can send a damaging email in error and immediately recognize your error and maybe, if all the stars line up, the email can be retrieved and deleted before anyone sees it, but that did not work so well with the gent with off color humor.

If there is no other option than responding to a sensitive issue than by email, compose the email in a word document to protect against inadvertently sending an initial draft of the response. Once the response is complete in word, wait before copying and pasting into an email to send. Wait, and possibly share the email with someone that can keep a confidence for an outsider's view of the correspondence. Wait long enough for any emotions to subside and then decide whether to copy and paste into an email document, modify the document, or simply send the response into the electronic trash.

If the email is in regard to disciplining a teammate, have someone in HR review the document before it is sent and only send it as a follow up to a face-to-face meeting with the individual. *The good thing about email is that it lasts forever*, when there is a possibility that it may be important to a future legal issue. Conversely, email correspondence is discoverable meaning that attorneys can demand access to that correspondence in certain circumstances. This is why no correspondence is trivial whether it be email, snail mail or text. If there is a conflict that must be documented, follow the instructions above regarding composing the email in a word document, have it reviewed by the appropriate parties, and then and only then, send the message.

If there is no company directive regarding the expected time to respond to email, then the leader should set a time limit of no more than 24 hours for non-emergency email and expect no less from other team members.

Phone conversations. Phone calls are best when face-to-face conversations are not possible. Both of the parties can get a sense of the emotions of the other party and can adjust the conversation accordingly. I once had a phone call with my boss in a corporate environment where what I said was not what I wanted to communicate and emotions flared; fortunately my boss was a perceptive person and recognized the call was not what either of us intended and told me it was time to hang up and that I should call back in ten minutes. It was a very long ten minutes, but both of us had a chance to reflect on what was said and we were able to get past that particular incident. Neither of us ever mentioned that call again.

This is an important lesson for leaders; when the conversation begins to go sideways, stop the call and take a break to reflect on what as just happened. Leaders should be able to compartmentalize issues and separate the heat of the moment and be willing to forget a momentary excursion from the way we normally conducted business.

There were no discoverable tracks from that phone call, but there may be circumstances where either party should make contemporaneous, (a nice legal term for jotting down the substance of the conversation, dating the note and keeping it for future reference (if necessary) notes. Contemporaneous notes may be legally accepted as evidence even if they are not shared with any other parties. In some very serious circumstances, the notes could be sent to oneself in snail mail, and then kept, unopened with a date stamp cancelation on the envelope, just in case they are required in the future.

The instances that may require this type of action may be when a senior leader instructs you to do a certain action that may not be overtly illegal, but with which you are not comfortable. Directions to commit an illegal act should be captured as well, but this will also trigger a consequential decision that may mean separation from the company or team. Sometimes HR policies may require a stepped discipline process starting with a verbal counseling session. While this first step is verbal, team leaders should keep time stamped notes of the conversation should additional personnel action be required.

Like emails, non-emergency phone messages should be responded to in a certain time period and if none is set by the company, then phone messages should be responded to by the end of the business day.

Text communications. Text communications are similar to email in that they can last forever, but usually the subject, at least in a business setting, is focused and able to be addressed in a few words. The same rules apply regarding addressing sensitive issues when composing a text and if there is anything other than a factual correspondence that could generate an emotional response, do not use text.

Response time for text messages should be similar to responding to phone messages.

Face to face meetings. Sometimes only a face-to-face meeting will do, and in this context, a face to face meeting may actually be face to face in an office or via a teleconferencing app.

Meetings should be time limited. When a request is made to meet, the request should include a desired time allotment to discuss the issue. The meeting request should also include the topic, again remember the meeting request may be discoverable, so even meeting requests should be carefully considered as they are composed.

Meetings should have all the relevant supporting information: charts, correspondence logs, photos, spreadsheets and so on, should be provided to the senior leader for their consideration, if time allows, prior to the meeting. In addition, the desired outcome of the meeting should be stated in order that the senior leader may be prepared to render a decision if needed.

Maintain communications for future reference. You never know when an obscure communication will rise to the top of the pile in importance. The challenge is how to file correspondence so there is any hope of retrieving it in a timely fashion. Paper files are still required for certain correspondence, but in an electronic age more is needed.

A Microsoft product called "One Note" is an excellent tool for leaders to keep information and correspondence. Similar products are available in other operating systems for those not having One Note, but for this purpose we will use the term "One Note". The program is easy to use, and there are a number of tutorials available for the novice user.

One Note is a great place to copy important emails, scans of paper correspondence, product literature, contemporaneous notes and much more. Information can be arranged based on the sender, a particular project, or any given topic and can be readily searched using key words. In a broad sense it is an electronic version of hanging files and file folders. Clutter can be eliminated and access improved, but the consideration remains that sensitive information (or any written correspondence in any format for that matter) stored in One Note is discoverable in a legal action and the decision must be made as to using One Note or not for a particular purpose.

Sensitive team information like payroll information or private communications should be stored in password protected documents. Even birthdays, home addresses, and other private information is subject to hacking and leaders should protect that information and train their team to do the same.

Considerations for any form of communication. Communication matters in any format. Consideration should be given to the parties involved; for example, men and women may process certain communication differently or there may be different cultures represented so that the person composing the correspondence should not assume certain phrases or references will be understood by all. If there are technical references that not all of the correspondents understand, extra care should be given to present the material in language common to all.

It is also important to recognize that if someone asks what time it is, the answer should not be instructions on how to build a clock. In other words, do not over complicate answers to questions. In some instances, responding to a question with a clarifying question may help focus a response.

Tell Back method. Another excellent response is to use the "tell back" method when communicating with others. This is a very simple technique where the receiver of a message tells back to the sender what they have heard. Senders are responsible for what they say, and receivers are responsible for what they hear and it should never be assumed those two things are the same. Each of us filter what we see and hear through our culture and experiences, so it is always good to hear back from others what they think you said.

Speak with authority. Leaders at any level should demonstrate confidence in their interactions with others. This, of course, assumes the leader has the technical or managerial expertise required; speaking with confidence about something you know little about really can go sideways very quickly. Be careful sharing opinions, after all everyone can have an opinion on a given subject, but when you have facts and examples and can build a compelling story, then there is strength in your communications.

I was fortunate enough to work on, and complete, a Master of Science degree in Management before moving into the corporate world of a Fortune 50 healthcare company. One thing that was emphasized over and again in that degree program was that people really did not want to hear what I thought or what my opinion was on a given subject, but rather had I done the research and/or gathered the data required to understand and communicate a problem and propose a solution.

Take the time to see what others, preferably those that have had their reviewed by their peers, have to say on a given topic. Don't stop with one paper or article, but look for other work that affirms a particular approach and for work that has a contravening result, all with the purpose of presenting an objective and well thought out topic. Obviously, the more critical or important the issue, the more time should be spent on research. This approach is the definition of speaking with authority.

Speaking with confidence literally is in regard to how leaders speak and present. Leaders should speak clearly and in a volume and tone that is appropriate to the setting. Military leaders are taught to speak from the diaphragm and this allows for a voice to carry over some distance and to gain the attention of others when necessary.

Record yourself speaking and work to avoid speaking too softly for the circumstances; no one at the table should have to strain to hear and understand what you say. Stand up straight, look people in the eye, and speak clearly; all things mothers usually tell their children as they grow up.

Public speaking is one of the things most people dread more than almost anything else, but leaders need to have that skill to lead. A terrific resource to build speaking skills is **Toastmasters International**. Toastmasters has chapters in many cities around the world with the stated purpose of preparing its members for public speaking. Toastmasters trains members to speak with confidence, in a stated period of time, and in a variety of settings.

Take solutions, not problems, to the boss. In almost every company culture except for the "top down" culture, the boss is really more interested in solutions than being depended on to solve subordinate leaders problems, after all that is why the boss hired subordinate leaders since there are larger "boss type" problems to be dealt with every day.

For those problems that fall directly within the job descriptions or within the work of the team, they should be solved by the subordinate leader and their team. From time to time, problems arise that really aren't in the job description and those are the problems that subordinate leaders should brainstorm for potential solutions and then prepare a brief problem statement followed by a proposed solution or potential solutions ranked in order. The magnitude of the problem should be noted and the cost/benefit of the desired solution presented. These types of problems will generally have an impact on the team budget.

Occasionally problems will surface between different teams within the organization that are not easily solved by negotiations between the affected team leaders. These types of problems are legitimate to bring to the boss, preferably with one or more potential solutions, for upper management to weigh in on with a solution. The caution in these circumstances is the solution the boss chooses may not be what either of the team leaders have considered and may be less desirable to one or both of the subordinate team leaders.

The key takeaway is when the team or team leaders of more than one team can come to a solution for the issue, the team leader(s) retains control of the issue. Once a problem is elevated up the chain, the subordinate team leaders have lost control of their own destiny in regards to the problem/solution decision. Problems should always be solved at the lowest level possible, where the most knowledge typically resides and the team will be less impacted by decisions made up the chain of command.

Deliver bad news without delay and good news as soon as possible. Seldom is news just news. When the leader fails on a particular issue, that piece of bad news will find it way to the corner office on the tenth floor at the speed of sound. Notice I said "when the leader fails" instead of when the team fails. Failure is something to be owned by the team leader, and no one is particularly interested in the excuse or excuses for the failure.

A simple "I really screwed up on this one" will go a long way in building your leadership legend, providing of course that you survive the failure. The boss almost always appreciates a simple admission and usually does not want to hear about how some team member didn't do their work. That was, after all, your job to ensure the work was done. Obviously, this is a face to face meeting, whenever possible, that needs to happen immediately.

Good news, on the other hand, can wait, but not so long it is no longer relevant. Good news is when the "we" part of leadership comes into play. Team members that made the most contributions to this good thing, should be singled out, but the entire team praised. This may seem a little incongruous with the admonition to blow your own horn, but this sharing of success will also become a part of the leadership legend. The right people will recognize who was ultimately responsible.

Be humble, but not too humble. I once had a very wise man tell me that if I did not blow my own horn occasionally, that someone else would come along and use it for a "urinal". The language was colorful, but the message was profound. Leaders should recognize their team when things go well and should be willing to accept criticism when the mark is missed. The challenge for a leader is to accept praise on behalf of their team, acknowledge their own contribution and to do these things without being arrogant and self-serving. Not a small challenge, but necessary to make sure the credit go where credit is due. Saying, "Aw shucks, it was nothing" may seem like a good response, but that response does neither the leader nor the team any service.

Pick your battles. This may seem to be a subject outside the topic of communication, but that is not necessarily so. Over the years I have observed leaders becoming so entrenched on an issue that actually led to their ultimate downfall. Leaders should always consider where their priorities fit with the organizations plan and the priorities of senior leaders and peer groups. Legal, moral and ethical consideration should be taken into account, and if none of those issues are present then the question should be asked by the leader if it is worth a battle when so many other issues may be present.

If legal, moral, and ethical issues are at play and there is no interest from senior leadership to address those issues, then a subordinate leader must make a decision that may have big consequences. First, is this the company that the leader wants to align themselves with? If the conclusion is no, then a carefully crafted resignation letter may be in order, but even then, the content and tone of the letter should be considered to cause the least amount of damage on the way out.

If the issues have legal implications or place others in jeopardy physically or financially, then the decision to act becomes even more critical. Leaders should always use the tools available to make a graduated complaint; many large organizations have an official within the organization that such issues may be discussed in confidence. If that is not available, then the choice is to confront senior leadership directly or to step outside the organization to government or regulatory agencies that may have jurisdiction, or simply do nothing at all. Of course the "do nothing" option will depend on the ethics of the leader.

Finally, no discussion on communications is complete without considering how the leader listens to others, and, in fact, active listening may be the most important part of communications. Active listening is more than just hearing and is the active process of decoding and understanding verbal messages. Active listeners tune out the other noise in their heads and concentrate on the message, and may interrupt the sender of the message to clarify what was just said. The "tell back" methodology addressed earlier, may be employed by the listener to "tell back" to the sender of the message what they have heard. Remember: "Speak with authority, listen with humility."

CONDUCTING EFFECTIVE MEETINGS

Effective meetings can be a powerful tool for teams, but too often drift away from the initial purpose of the meeting and run over time or simply do not accomplish the purpose set by the scheduler of the meeting. Poorly run meetings can even become a barrier to good workmanship.

One structure of an effective meeting includes the following elements: a leader, a time keeper, a note keeper, ideally a small group of no more than five to seven participants, a set agenda of two or three specific items including a time for each specific time, and next steps if the agenda items are not resolved during the meeting or new agenda items for the next meeting. This format may not be appropriate for every meeting or may need to be modified for meetings in a union environment, but it is very effective for working meetings intended to come to specific conclusions.

Meeting leader. The meeting leader is not necessarily intended to be the team leader and is best if this duty is passed around the meeting attendees. This may help to develop ownership of the team in the meeting and experience builds confidence and capabilities in conducting meetings.

The meeting leader's job is not to dominate the group, but rather to keep the meeting on track and on subject. Appointed leaders (asking for volunteers for the next scheduled meeting for the three positions of leader, record keeper and time keeper is desirable) should ensure the meeting room is prepared and required meeting documents or supplies, are available and send reminders to meeting members regarding any work they are to contribute to the meeting. During the meeting, action items for various topics may be identified and it is the leader's responsibility to ask for volunteers or appoint a team member to work on the action item and report back. The meeting leader should also ensure the assignment for leader, time keeper and note keeper are filled for the next meeting. Other duties may be identified from time to time.

The time keeper's job is to keep the meeting on time. When agenda items are added there should always be time identified for the discussion. Assuming the meeting is limited to one hour, recommended for most regularly scheduled meetings. The agenda may look like this and should be written on an easel pad to allow room for notes to be captured:

- *Monthly Quality Meeting*
- *Today's date*
- *Introductions and opening comments 5 minutes*
- *Topic number 1-15 minutes*
- *Topic number 2-20 minutes*
- *Topic number 3-15 minutes*
- *Closing, set agenda for next meeting including leadership assignment 5 minutes*

The time keeper is to remind the group when there is one minute left for discussion and then remind the group that time is up for that topic. The group can always choose to add more time or give back time for a particular topic, but the overall goal of one hour (or whatever meeting duration was set by the group) is intended to be honored.

Well conducted meetings that do not waste a participant's time are a benefit for all team members.

The record keeper or scribe captures the progress and results of the meeting. This important task ensures the team has the information from one meeting to the next to make effective progress on the assigned topics. Consider the use of an easel and full-sized tablets along with colored markers to capture the discussion in the meeting. Easel pads with a self-stick strip on the back allows the note keeper to post real time notes in full view of the team. The team can make corrections as required during the meeting.

Remember the who, what, when, where, and how questions when tasks are assigned to a team member. Every task should be time bound with an expected delivery date for the results. The notes can be captured by photo and shared to the team, but regardless of how that information is shared, a record of the progress should be kept for later reference.

One Note is a Microsoft product that facilitates capturing all relevant meeting material and catalog that information for easy retrieval later. Similar Apple products may exist for the same function.

Team members should commit to team participation and agree to take their turn in the various leadership positions on the team. They should also commit up front to complete any assigned tasks developed by the group.

Some teams actually make the creation of a charter for the group the first order of business. The charter may include the overarching goal of the team, objectives to be met, time frames to be met, a commitment to attend scheduled meetings, and a commitment to complete assigned tasks. The charter, usually a page or less, should then be signed by all participants. If a person cannot commit to the team charter, then that person should not be on the team.

Depending on the nature of the objective of the meeting or series of meetings, a final report detailing recommendations should be prepared for upper management. Cost of the recommendations should be estimated as well as the potential benefit. Time to implement the recommendations and anticipated time to expect a return on investment should be a part of the report.

Some projects may take a significant amount of time to complete as well as effort from team members. Team leaders should always remember to celebrate the completion of a significant task. Never overlook the opportunity to recognize others for good work.

Meeting supplies include, but are not limited to, the following:

- Easel
- Easel pad with self-adhesive pages
- Colored markers
- Note pads for the group
- Handouts, reading material, on-line sources

NEGOTIATIONS, PART OF LEADERSHIP

Negotiating may be a topic we don't think of often, but in reality we use those skills on a regular basis with team member, vendors and even the boss. One approach I like to use, regardless of the type of subject matter, is to develop three desirable outcomes for a particular negotiation, which I usually keep to myself:

- <u>Best case</u> outcome where you can get everything you ask without much or any pushback
- <u>Desirable</u> outcome that yields a satisfactory result and may require some give and take during the negotiations
- <u>Walk-away</u> outcome which is the result at which your needs, or the needs of the team, are not met and there is no benefit in further negotiations

Outcomes could be wage increases, benefits, better vendor or supplier deals or negotiations to resolve conflicts that were discussed earlier. The point is that one should never enter negotiations on any subject without considering the desired outcomes or the point at which you figuratively or literally walk away. To do any less is to place yourself in a weakened position from the start.

Negotiations in the context of a team or organization tend to be one of two types: distributive negotiation and integrative negotiation.

Distributive negotiation is where the team sits down at the table to decide how a beautiful apple pie will be cut and shared with the team members. Is the pie cut and served based on the size of the recipient or by how much work a particular individual contributed to picking the apples or baking the pie?

In this type of negotiation, someone will need to lose or give up something of value to another team member. This is not necessarily the best type of negotiation to be a part of, but may be forced into from time to time.

Integrative negotiations, on the other hand, deal with situations where there may be several issues on the table and where each party may place more value or less value on the various parts of the negotiation than others at the same table.

This particular circumstance may allow a more equitable result where one party is willing to relinquish a less important issue to gain benefit on something more important.

Integrative negotiating is a more open process where the first step of all the parties is to clearly state their various interests and begin to identify the things both parties can readily agree on. Once the common goals are established, then the parties can begin to discuss various options and propose potential deals for consideration. Each party analyzes the other parties' proposals and work together to tweak the various proposals where both parties achieve a desirable (not necessarily best case or ideal) outcome.

Once both parties to the negotiations are satisfied they have a workable outcome, then the process should be put in writing with signatures from both parties. Successful outcomes can prove to be a model for future negotiations. Negotiations of this type are sometimes identified as value-added negotiation.

Integrative negotiations are only possible if a leader is self-confident, willing to display some vulnerability, and willing to trust others in the negotiations. There will be occasions where that trust may be misplaced, but where both parties are able to freely express themselves, it may be the beginning of a lasting, positive relationship.

MANAGING CONFLICT

If you are in a leadership position, sooner or later some conflict will arise that must be addressed. It is a fact of modern life that conflict will present at the most inopportune time. Conflict left un-addressed will likely fester and grow until the solution is much more unpleasant and difficult to deal with than when first discovered. Lack of conflict may even be undesirable in that it may be an indicator of apathy, burnout, or any of a number of unhealthy factors that impact the effectiveness of a team.

There are generally two types of conflict that leaders need to be aware of on their team or within their organization: functional conflict and dysfunctional conflict. [1]

Functional conflictThis is the type of conflict that can expose a weak spot in a team and, when addressed properly, will bring a positive solution to the entire team. Desired outcomes of functional conflict are agreement, improved relationships and learning. Dysfunctional conflict. This is the type of conflict that negatively impacts the team or organizations performance. This type of conflict has no positive resolution and must be eradicated quickly in order not to damage the team.

Personality conflicts are certainly one type of conflict that can surface in a team. These types of conflicts can spring up from something as simple as a personal habit that irritates a team member. Over time, the squeaky chair or the drumming of a pencil can drive the person in the next cubicle crazy. Civility in daily life has certainly taken a hit in recent years and that definitely impacts team members that may spend more time with each other during the day than with family. Bad things can and do come from this emerging lack of civility.

Leaders cannot ignore the emergent dynamics of the team and must be vigilant to recognize cycles of incivility that may be developing and be ready to break that cycle immediately. Leaders that become aware of conflict within the team should:

- Investigate and document the conflict
- Provide feedback or counseling to the affected parties
- Attempt an informal dispute resolution

If all else fails, consider referring the matter to your immediate boss or HR. Another possibility is to bring in outside counselors or mediators to attempt resolution.

None of this is to be taken lightly. Think about workplace violence and do not assume that cannot manifest in your team. Take action and make sure you have a graduated response that is approved by HR or legal counsel.

The multi-ethnic and multi-cultural makeup of the workforce is another potential source of conflict. The challenge here is to work to develop cross cultural relationships and understandings of how others with different backgrounds think and feel.

For leaders, this starts with the same active listening mentioned earlier in this book. Other important actions are to be sensitive to others and learn, as much as is possible, about their customs, build rapport by asking questions about cultural differences.

I once met two Afghan men on a train who worked in the construction trades in the US. Their dress was different, but their English was good and we talked for an hour or two about our families. We did not solve the problems of the world, but I think each of us went away from that conversation perhaps felling that we had just a little bit more in common that we thought. It is worth the effort to reach out and to help avoid needless conflict in multi-cultural teams. [1]

BALANCING WORK, SELF, AND HOME

Along with all the other things a leader must consider are the compartmentalization of work, self and home. Compartmentalization of these three elements of life is not always possible or even necessary, but in most cases should at least be understood.

Work is important for so many reasons. Work provides the basic needs of an individual or family and the potential for achieving a desirable lifestyle. Work may provide a sense of accomplishment and a source of pride. The danger in work is the potential to easily slide into the habit where work eclipses the other important aspects of life.

Once, many years ago when I was CEO of my construction company and also in my terminal assignment as Commander of a Field Artillery Battalion, I found myself spiraling out of control and knew that I was in a very unhealthy situation. A typical work day started at 6:30 in the morning so I could get a few hours of calm before the phone started ringing and ended at 6:00 p.m. when I left the office for home. Weekends in the National Guard would find me driving as much as 500 miles and spending as much as 36 hours on task in a two day weekend or occasionally flying out of state for meetings; typically there were two weekends committed to the military and on occasion as many as all weekends in a month were committed that time. On the weekends I was home, Saturday was a six-hour work day. Thanksgiving morning and other holidays offered a change for some quiet time to catch up on business.

At that time there was a group that offered seminars with the purpose of increasing self-awareness. I won't go into the details of the long weekend, but one assignment was to write my own obituary. This was scheduled for about 2 a.m. after a very long day, I think the hour was purposely late in order to bring the participants close to the edge of their endurance when emotions begin to run hot. It was a humbling experience to take the time to consider what those few lines in the newspaper would look like especially considering the lack of balance in my life. Take some uninterrupted time to craft your own obituary as your life is today and then think about what you would like it to truthfully say at the end of your story.

There were several inflection points during my life where my wife and I spent a week on the beach or at a cabin in the mountains with no television, no phone, and no interruptions, specifically for the purpose of examining where we were at that time and where we wanted to be in ten years. I still have the handwritten notes from a weekend in the mountains and later from the beach in Corpus Christi decades ago. Did we accomplish everything we thought we should focus on? No, but we were about 80% to 90% successful.

The things we talked about included finances, where we wanted to live, what we wanted to do in our leisure time and when we wanted retirement to look like. One thing I heard that impressed me was the admonition to begin with the end in mind, so I started buying books for 40 and 50 somethings to consider for retirement and began taking a newsletter on investing and retirement. When is the right time to start this type of introspection? The answer, of course is right now, but sometimes life gets in the way. The early years and then years raising a family make it really tough for introspection, so you have to be very intentional and put a high priority on setting a few days aside away from distractions to think about who you, or we as a married couple, wanted to be if we were blessed with the years to grow old.

One of the most important things a leader, or anyone else for that matter, should consider is personal well-being. Leaders lead by example, and that includes a physical example of maintaining their own health as medical conditions allow (never begin a workout program without consulting a physician). A regular regime of physical activity is beneficial in a number of ways; leaders that are more physically fit can better withstand the rigors of work and everyday life in addition to raising their level of wellness. Over the years, I was fortunate enough to be able to take a mid-day break for run or strength workout. Most of the time this was over a lunch period, but it was refreshing to return to work with even a brief workout.

A 30-minute walk or run with a 30-minute weight program on alternating days proved beneficial for me. I first consulted my physician to understand any physical limitation that may exist then I spent about $100 or so for a personal trainer to develop a program appropriate for my age and fitness level. I am convinced that maintaining a reasonable level of fitness allowed me to bring my best at work and that allowed me to provide for my family.

Personal life may be every bit as challenging as work in that when work and the worries of the day ride home in the passenger seat of the car, they may become an unwelcome guest at the dinner table. For those that are the boss at work, it can be challenging to understand they may not be the boss at home. My wife has explained this to me any number of times, and I continue to require an occasional tune up in this regard.

I once attended a seminar and remember the speaker building an image of an imaginary tree in front of the house belonging to an individual returning home from a very demanding day at work. The image was of a person pausing before they reached the steps to their house to unload the day and hang it on the branches of the tree, left for the night to be re-shouldered in the morning. It didn't always work that way with me, and it is much more difficult in a much more accessible world, but there are boundaries that may be considered to help break the blur between self, work and life at home.

A boundary may be establishing limits on reading and returning email, texts, or taking phone calls at home. If you happen to be in a leadership position that can influence policy, spelling out the expectations of such a boundary and when an emergency requires the boundary line to be crossed. If you do decide that email and text will not be responded to after a certain hour, then it is important to communicate those expectations to others and to encourage those boundaries be adopted by all.

Time alone in meditation or prayer at the beginning of every day allows for a mental reset. The great religions all have some sort of admonition to clear ones thoughts and consider that there may be a greater purpose that is established for each of us. In 2023, Gen Z is leaving organized religion at an astonishing rate for a variety of reasons. For those that have read the Christian Bible, there is a story about a man occupied by a legion of evil spirits. The gist of the story was that the evil spirits could be cast out, but something else would soon occupy that empty space. I am not a theologian or psychologist, but I have observed that it seems that people tend to have some sort of religion, even if they are adamant there is no place in their life for that sort of thing. The possible question to consider is, "Are those things that I am doing emptying my spirit or refreshing my spirit?" It is up to each of us to decide.

TIME MANAGEMENT

You may know this person: always busy and dealing with crisis at every turn, a company hero with sweat dropping from their brow with a stack of paper on the desk and sticky notes surrounding the perimeter of the computer monitor like petals on a daisy. The counterpoint to this individual is the person that quietly goes about their day and yet somehow never misses a deadline and is the go-to person for dealing with real emergencies.

A professor once was lecturing his class on how to fit everything into a busy schedule. For a demonstration, he had several large rocks, more medium sized rocks, many smaller ones, a jar of sand and a large glass jar. He first asked the class if they thought everything would fit in the jar at one time and received mixed answers so he proceeded to his demonstration by pouring the sand in the jar, followed by the small rocks, then medium and finally the large rocks. The demonstration failed when the large rocks would not fit completely in the jar.

After some discussion, the professor took everything back out of the jar and proceeded to fill it in reverse order, first with the big rocks, then medium rocks, then small rocks, and finally pouring the sand over the top. The sand was fine enough that it found its way between the spaces in the big rocks, then the medium rocks and finally filled all the space between the small rocks. And everything fit.

The point of the demonstration is to manage those big important critical items first, then the second tier of issues, then the third and finally those small things that are continually present will find an appropriate place in the jar.

IMPORTANT AND URGENT

An important facet of leadership is developing the ability to recognize the difference between urgent issues and important issues.

The dictionary definition of important is "something of great significance or value; likely to have a profound effect on success, survival or well-being." Urgent is defined as something requiring immediate action or attention. An example of an important issue would be the final paper that is due at a certain place and certain time for a continuing education class that will be the final qualification for a substantial raise. The urgent situation would be the unexpected car breakdown or appliance failure that will impact the entire family. A difficult choice on where to spend valuable time before a deadline.

One sure thing about both important and urgent issues is that they will affect the team and possibly the entire organization. Leaders must consider the questions below and develop a communication plan on how the important and/or urgent issues is to be resolved. If the issues cannot be corrected immediately, consider regular updates to the affected parties along with assistance to develop mitigating plans for those impacted. <u>The importance of clear and regular communications</u>

cannot be understated; most people are willing to forgive an inconvenience if they are told the truth and kept informed.

QUESTIONS TO RESOLVE

Is the issue both important and urgent? This issue may be very difficult to deal with but choosing the priority for action is fairly obvious. Failure to act will jeopardize not only the next moment, but the long term objectives of the organization.

Is the issue important but not urgent? This issue is one that must be resourced and monitored, but which may be suspended briefly due to an emergency. Briefly is the qualifier, in that as soon as possible the work is taken back up on this important work.

Is the issue urgent but not important? Urgent but not important? This is the type of issue that can be delegated or contracted out to an outside entity with the customer or impacted party notified as to how the issue will be resolved and regular monitoring required.

Is the issue neither important nor urgent? These types of items can stay on the "to do" list for a long time to be addressed when resources are available, or maybe just discarded if there is no impact at all to the goals, objectives, and tactics important to the strategic plan.

Don't forget to address the "who, what, why, when, where, and how" details and don't forget that others may be impacted downstream from the team. Who are these people and what does the issue mean to their important work. Lean on the boss for another viewpoint of who an urgent issue may impact.

The truth is that urgent issues will always crop up and require immediate attention while important issues must not be left to languish.

UNDERSTAND YOURSELF AND UNDERSTAND OTHERS

The human resource issues discussed above are not comprehensive and there will always be unique events or circumstances that require a leader to be empathetic, steadfast, tough, or gentle. The key is to be aware of those things that everyday life brings to work and to understand your people, and even more so, to understand yourself.

There are any number of psychological tools available to leadership to help understand the various personality types that make up a team. Perhaps one of the best known tools is the Myers-Briggs personality test that will help the leader and the employee better understand personality types and assist in developing expectations. While there is a charge for the Myers-Brigs test, 16 Personalities is available online at www.16personalities.com and should provide a satisfactory result. Other personality tests may be very effective, including the DiSC Profile Personality Tool, along with several others. The reader should examine which tool provides the best value for their organization. Traits and examples listed below are a brief overview suggested by the 16 Personalities site.

The online self-test usually takes less than fifteen minutes or so. A leader can build their team in the 16 Personalities portal and then complete their own self-assessment, then the team can access the site for their opportunity to conduct a personality assessment. The leader can then view the reports of the personal and team assessments, and finally, the 16 Personalities site offers various self-directed workshops for the leader to share with their team. Results of the test will be presented in a four-letter format using a series of letters that identify the personality type.

Generally speaking, Meyers-Brigs will help the individual discover in which of the four main psychological types their personalities lie and further dive down into detail within the four major personality types for greater detail. Each major personality is usually further divided into two different manifestations of the combination of personality traits. <u>Remember that people are very complex and there can be overlap in personality types, but predominate traits should emerge</u>. It is also very important to remember tshat the percentage of traits shown below is not equally distributed between males and females. The reader should visit the 16 Personalities website for more detail, but a brief recap follows below. The estimated percentages may not total exactly to 100% because the estimated percentages, like people, do not fit precisely into a neat box.

WHY PERSONALITIES MATTER

Why do personality types matter? If you study and understand the different personalities, (the 16 Personalities site has much more detail regarding each personality type), then the leader may be able to avoid a mismatch in hiring members for the team. None of the personality types are inherently good or bad, but not all personality types belong on the same team based on the expected outcomes of the team. Selecting the wrong personality type can mean failure for the individual and disruption of the team.

The four major categories are: <u>Analysts, Diplomats, Sentinels, and Explorers</u>.

Analysts present in four general categories

INTJ: The Architect. This is a rare personality type with the following traits
- Introverted, Intuitive, Thinking, and Judging, about 2% of the population
- Generally rational and quick witted
- Independent thinkers
- Quick to see through phoniness and hypocrisy
- Tireless evaluation of the world around them-a trait that can wear on others

- Questioning everything and making their own rules
- Single minded desire for success
- Not warm and fuzzy personalities
- Think Elon Musk

INTP: The Logician
- Introverted, Intuitive, Thinking, and Prospecting, about 3% to 5% of the population
- May seem to be off in their own world
- Likes understand patterns
- Quickly spot irregularities and dishonesty
- May overthink even small decisions
- Think Albert Einstein

ENTJ: The Commander
- Extraverted, Intuitive, Thinking, and Judging, about 2% of the population
- Decisive personality
- Love momentum and accomplishment
- Gather information and act
- Natural born leader with particular skill to recognize talent in others
- May make others uncomfortable in the drive to make things happen
- Loves a challenge
- Think Steve Jobs or Margaret Thatcher

ENTP: The Debater
- Extraverted, Intuitive, Thinking, and Prospecting, about 2% to 5% of the population
- Bold and creative
- Quick witted and outspoken
- Rebellious streak

- Great Devil's Advocate
- Can be uncomfortable as they tend to pick ideas apart
- Think Mark Twain

Diplomats present in four different personalities

INFJ: The Advocate
- Introverted, Intuitive, Feeling and Judging, about 1% to 3% of the population
- Idealistic and principled
- Big goals and ambitions
- Clear sense of values
- Sense of being different from others, but able to build relationships
- Think of Martin Luther King or Mother Teresa

INFP: The Mediator
- Introverted, Intuitive, Feeling, and Prospecting, about 4% of the population
- Creative and imaginative
- Idealistic and empathetic
- Tuned into their own thoughts
- May be overwhelmed by need to correct their perceived need to fight injustice
- Need a sense of purpose
- Think of Shakespeare or J.R.R. Tolkien

ENFJ: The Protagonist
- Extraverted, Intuitive, Feeling, and Judging, about 2.5% of the population
- Feel call to "do the right thing"
- Born leaders, many are politicians, teachers, or coaches
- Vocal about values

- Like to solve other people problems
- Think of Barack Obama or Oprah Winfrey

ENFP: The Campaigner
- Extraverted, Intuitive, Feeling and Prospecting, about 8% of the population
- Free spirits
- Like to build relationships
- Infectious personality
- May be difficult to focus
- May be disorganized
- Think of Robert Downey, Jr. or Robin Williams

Sentinels present in four different personalities

ISTJ: The Logistician
- Introverted, Observant, Thinking, and Judging, about 13 % of the population
- Live a life of integrity
- Reliable and practical
- Like structure and tradition
- Strong work ethic, but are disturbed when they perceive others do not share their belief
- Think Angela Merkel or Denzel Washington

ISFJ: The Defender
- Introverted, Observant, Feeling, and Judging, about 14% of the population
- Make the world go round
- Meets deadlines
- Can do personality
- Loyal
- May be perfectionist
- Need recognition

- Think of Queen Elizabeth II or Dr. Watson—sidekick to Sherlock Holmes

ESTJ: The Executive, 8% to 12% of the population
- Extraverted, Observant, Thinking, and Judging
- Stabilizing force
- Like tradition and order
- Like bringing people together
- Certain of their knowledge even against heavy resistance
- Think of John D. Rockefeller or Judge Judy

ESFJ: The Consul, about 12% of the population
- Extraverted, Observant, Feeling, and Judging
- Like hospitality and good manners
- Believe in giving back and doing the right thing
- May struggle when others disagree with with them
- Loyal and build lasting relationships
- Think of Bill Clinton or Taylor Swift

Explorers present in four different personalities

ISTP: The Virtuoso
- Introverted, Observant, Thinking, and Prospecting, about 5% of the population
- Love to explore by seeing and touching
- Makers and Craftsmen/ women
- Love to troubleshoot problems
- Sometimes unpredictable
- Think of Bear Grylls or Clint Eastwood

ISFP: The Adventurer
- Introverted, Observant, Feeling, and Prospecting, about 5% of the population

- True artists
- Unassuming and humble, just doing their own thing
- Flexible and adaptable
- May have trouble with long term plans
- Live in the present
- Think of Bob Dylan or Kevin Costner

ESTP: The Entrepreneur
- Extraverted, Observant, Thinking, and Prospecting. about 4% to 6% of the population
- Like to be center of attention
- Leap before they look
- May be impatient with formal education
- Walk a thin line between success and failure
- Think of Ernest Hemingway or Bruce Willis

ESFP: The Entertainer
- Extraverted, Observant, Feeling, and Prospecting, about 9% of the population
- Live life in the moment
- Very social
- Complex and repetitive tasks are boring
- May be poor planners
- Think Marilyn Monroe or Elton John

What happens if there is no opportunity for an individual to take the 16 Personalities assessment?

Personal observation of the individual, posture, facial expressions, and body language can come into play. DISCinsights.com offers guidance on how to approximate personality types based on observation.

Is it proper to use personality test or observations to help understand how an individual may fit in an organization?

Arguments exist that caution about using the various personality test during hiring. Even the Meyers-Briggs Foundation questions the ethics of using their test during the hiring process. Generally, the question of ethics is based on the fact that the tests were developed for a particular culture, and in many countries, there are multiple cultures present in the work force. The reader should understand that the personality test is only a tool and the efficacy of that tool may be skewed one way or another by the background the individual raised in a different culture.

At the end of the day, the leader must decide based on their observations from interviews, personality tests, specific job requirements, and recommendations of references. This is what leaders do; sometimes the messages are mixed for reasons that are not clear, but it is the leader's job to make a decision. That decision may be yes, no, not now, or keep looking, but the decision should not be delayed, and the message delivered sooner rather than latter and with the appropriate feedback when allowed.

HEROS AND GOATS

There is no formula that people are plugged into with the resulting proof that they are a card carrying leader. Unlike technical certifications that confer a certain title or honor on an individual, certifications and degrees are wonderful things that provide tangible proof of achieving a certain milestone; leadership on the other hand, is something that people know when they see it. Think back about great leaders you have read about or learned about through family stories handed down generation to generation.

Inspirational leadership may be a bit like a Purple Heart in the military. The Purple Heart is awarded to those that have been injured in action. Some injuries are relatively minor and some are grievous, but a common preference is to never have suffered the injury at all rather than be a recipient of this high honor. The following examples of great leaders have one thing in common, they paid for their recognition with pain of one sort or another. I have to say that Chamberlain is my personal hero. I've read the books and stood at the top of Little Round Top at Gettysburg. I tried to imagine what that July day was like and wondered what I might have done in the same circumstance, and hope that that introspection has made me a more effective leader, but there are so many historical examples, and a few current examples, to consider if you choose to name one as a hero to be emulated.

It is good to have heroes, they are different for everyone, but here are a few that have left a lasting impression on me. As you read, consider the leadership skills discussed in the previous chapter.

JOSHUA CHAMBERLAIN

Joshua Chamberlain was an American college professor from Maine during the Civil War. Chamberlain left his position at the school for a sabbatical, and immediately volunteered for the Union Army. His education, and possibly reputation, offered him a position in the officer Corps and command of the 2nd Maine. He led his troops in a number of battles, but perhaps the most consequential was the battle of Little Round Top at Gettysburg in July of 1863.

One excellent accounting of that particular battle is in the book "Killer Angels" by Michael Shaara and is recommended reading for those that want more information about that day.

Chamberlin was given the task to occupy the strategic hill known as Little Round Top and arrived in that location directly from a long and arduous march literally a few minutes before the battle began. The significance of Little Round Top was that it was on the very flank, or end, of the Union Army and, had it fallen, would have created a serious vulnerability to the entire Union Army.

It is interesting to note that while on the march, he was given a number of Maine deserters that became a liability as the position was hastily occupied.

Just moments after he had arrayed his soldiers at the top of the hill, ten or fifteen minutes according to some historians, a rebel unit attacked and were repulsed by Chamberlin's soldiers at the loss of a number of his men. Moments later there was a second charge up the hill and again the attack was repulsed with further losses. So many losses that Chamberlain ordered the deserters to fill in holes opened in the line. There was a third charge up the hill and Chamberlain, who had been walking along the top of the hill directing the action, ordered his troops to fix bayonets and charge down the hill to thwart what turned out to be the last effort of that day.

Chamberlain was shot in the boot and his canteen while directing his unit, but gained the respect of his men, including the deserters, the commanders over him and his opponents on the battle field. When General Lee eventually surrendered, he requested that Chamberlain be the Officer to receive his sword.

Chamberlain, Medal of Honor recipient, was eventually promoted to the rank of General, served as the Governor of Maine, and president of Bowden College. He died in 1914 in Portland Maine.

Chamberlin's conviction, courage, education, compassion, and empathy moved me when I first read of his place in history, but he is not the only person that demonstrated great leadership.

MOTHER TERESA

Mother Teresa was born in Albania in 1910 and, while in her teens, chose to become a Catholic Nun and dedicate her life to service, leaving home at the age of 18 to never see her mother or sister again. In 1950 she was moved by the extreme poverty in Calcutta, India and left her position in a Catholic school she had held since 1946 to serve the poor that so moved her. In 1950 she founded the "Missionaries of Charity", a religious order that others with the same vision soon joined. She later wrote about her decision in 1946 to leave the relative comfort of the school and begin her work of service to the poor. She experienced what she later described as "the call within the call" which led her to believe that she was to "leave the Convent and help the poor while living among them. It was an order. To fail would have been to break the faith".

She replaced her traditional habit, or dress, with a simple white cotton Indian Sari with a blue border to signify this new commitment. After some basic medical training, she was joined on her mission by a group of young women committed to the service of the poorest of the poor. Later in 1952, she opened a hospice to comfort the dying poor. Mother Teresa said, "A beautiful death is for people who lived like animals to die like angels-loved and wanted."

The hospice was in a converted Hindu temple where those of all faiths were brought to "die with dignity according to their faith; Muslims were read the Quran, Hindus received water from the Ganges, and Catholics received extreme unction"(quoted from Wikipedia). Later she opened a hospice for those with leprosy, established leprosy outreach clinics, and outside of hospice and clinical care, began to take in an increasing number of homeless children.

By the year of her death in 1997, the thirteen-member Calcutta congregation grew to over 4,000 Catholic Sisters working worldwide. She said, "By blood, I am Albanian. By citizenship, an Indian. By faith, I am a Catholic nun. As to my calling, I belong to the world. As to my heart, I belong entirely to the Heart of Jesus." (Quoted from Wikipedia).

I met people like Mother Teresa during my time in healthcare. As I visited the 100 or so hospitals nationwide that were, in small part, my responsibility I found another nameless example that left me speechless. It was a winter day in Little Falls, Minnesota, and during my tour of the hospital, the local facility director insisted I visit the facility's shop where painters, carpenters, plumbers, electricians and others worked every day to create and maintain a safe space for patients and staff.

It was a project the carpenter had on the workbench that particularly moved me. At first it seemed to be a box, but on further examination, it was a simple wooden casket for one of the elderly nuns that would soon pass away. The facility staff had responsibility for many things, one of which was a home for elderly nuns that had come to the end of a life of service. The facility director told me that they were not allowed to line the casket with any cloth and they even had to remove the carrying handles before the casket was lowered into the grave, dug by the facility staff, because that would have been an "extravagance" and that hardware could be used on the next simple pine box the carpenter would build when the time came.

These women poured out their life much like Mother Teresa with no fanfare, no awards, and no reward except for the one they expected at God's hand.

ROSA PARKS

Rosa Parks, born Rosa Louise McCauley Parks on February 4th 1913, grew up in the segregated South in Montgomery Alabama. The city bus system had an established practice of placing a sign part way back in the bus to separate the white section from the colored section. It is important to note the sign was moved from its usual position after the third or fourth row further back in the bus if the "white" section filled up and those sitting in that row were expected to give up their seat and move further back in the bus. This is a concept difficult to grasp in 2022 but was accepted by both black and white riders as a given fact up until December the 1st, 1955; the day that Rosa Parks decided that she had had enough and, instead of moving to a row further back, chose to simply slide toward the window side of the seat.

Rosa Parks was not the first to protest this practice of segregation, but she was the perfect person at that particular time to be the face of the movement to end racial segregation. Her decision on that fateful day led to her arrest. She later said, "When that white driver stepped back toward us, when he waved his hand and ordered us up and out of our seats, I felt a determination cover my body like a quilt on a winter night." Rosa was one of four sitting in that row and the other three left their seats and moved. She was arrested for her insubordination and breaking a 1900 city ordnance regarding segregation. Months after her arrest she said in an interview, that she had decided "I would have to know for once and for all what rights I had as a human being and a citizen." She was later tried and found guilty in a 30-minute trial where she was fined $10 and $4 in court costs.

Rosa Parks was seen as a responsible, mature woman with a good reputation. She was securely married and employed, was regarded as possessing a quiet and dignified demeanor, and was politically savvy. Martin Luther King said that Parks was regarded as "one of the finest citizens of Montgomery-not one of the finest Negro citizens, but one of the finest citizens of Montgomery" (quoted form Wikipedia).

At her death on October 24, 2005, at the age of 92, her body was transported from Detroit to Washington D.C. to lie in honor in the rotunda of the U.S. Capitol, a special tribute to a special person.

Over the years, I had the privilege to associate with many people of different education, color, ethnicity, faith, and cultural backgrounds and I never failed to be surprised that for the most part, we were all just people trying our best to make a better life for self and family. I've learned that sometimes the hero appears when the need presents, and it just may be the most unassuming person you know that makes the decision to stand up for what is right.

ABRAHAM LINCOLN

Abraham Lincoln may be the most revered Presidents of the United States of all time, and is consistently ranked in the top three and often as number one by various surveys, with George Washington and Franklin Roosevelt close behind.

All three, Lincoln, Washington, and Roosevelt, faced enormous challenges, but it fell to Lincoln to protect the union that was not yet 100 years old. At the time of his presidency, he may have been one of the most loved and most hated holders of the office. He took office in a period of fear and high anxiety and, in his first inaugural speech gave every indication that he thought war could be avoided when he said, "We are not enemies, but friends. We must not be enemies. Though passion may have strained, it must not break our bonds of affection." That would soon change.

It is very interesting to note the makeup of the Presidential Cabinet which he began to construct on election night and included all his main rivals for the Republican nomination and therefore had just lost the election to Lincoln. According to Wikipedia, Lincoln "did not shy away from surrounding himself with strong minded men, even those whose credentials for office appeared to be much more impressive than his own."

William Seward, although deeply disappointed by his loss to Lincoln, was offered and accepted the position of Secretary of State. Seward became the dominate figure of the cabinet and remained in that office for the duration of Lincoln's time in office. Seward not only served during a time of great distress, but negotiated the acquisition of the Alaska Territory as well.

Seward was followed by several others, but possibly most notable was the appointment of Edwin Stanton as Secretary of War (now Secretary of Defense), who replaced Simon Cameron in the lead up to the Civil War. Stanton was a Democrat and ended up working very closely and likely more often with Lincoln than any other cabinet member due to the war.

It may have been far easier to appoint likeminded thinkers to the Cabinet and to find weaker souls that would not speak up and oppose the President, but Lincoln recognized the value of dissenting voices when making consequential decisions.

For a deep dive into the appointments and relationships of the Lincoln Cabinet, see *Team of Rivals: The Political Genius of Abraham Lincoln*.

It seems that Lincoln holds a special place in history. He stood at the crossroads when this experiment we know as America was about to be ripped apart like yesterday's newspaper as a fire starter. What a burden to think about the soldiers he sent in harm's way, many never to return. What brilliance to bring together a team of rivals to conduct the most important conflict this nation has ever stood since it was conceived? What an example for leaders as they build their teams for whatever work is set before them.

GEORGE ARMSTRONG CUSTER

George Armstrong Custer was born December 5th, 1839 and died, along with 267 of the soldiers entrusted to his command and an unknown number of Indian warriors, on June the 25th, 1876. There were unthinkable atrocities from all sides during the war with the Plaines Indians after the Civil War, and there is no intent to attribute right or wrong from that day, only to examine the actions of the leader of the soldiers lost that day. The Sioux, Cheyenne and others suffered great loss as well, but they recovered their dead and that number is unknown.

I have walked the battle site at the Little Big Horn and have to say it is especially somber and has a haunted air. The battlefield is dotted with stone markers where the soldiers fell and one can almost imagine the disintegration of five trained Companies of Cavalry into final defensive positions as the Army broke under the weight of superior forces.

Controversies surround that day and the events leading up to Custer's defeat on that hot summer day, and the reader is encouraged to read more about this massive failure that resonates over 145 years later. Some blame subordinate commanders like Major Reno and Captain Benteen for the loss, but Custer made decisions leading up to the battle that cemented the outcome.

He divided his 600 soldier command and took only 257 into battle in the face of superior numbers of Sioux and Cheyenne warriors numbering somewhere between as few as 1,000 to more than 1,800 based on various accounts.

He refused an offer of support of four additional companies of soldiers four days before the battle saying "[I[could whip any Indian village on the Plains" with his own regiment and the additional soldiers "would only be a burden".

He chose to leave behind his battery of Gatling Guns even knowing he was facing superior numbers. Custer chose speed over the slower travel of the Gatlin Guns on that fateful day.

He had his troops, including his officers, box their sabers and send them to the rear before the battle.

President Grant, a seasoned leader of the Union Army in the Civil War was quoted in the *New York Herald* on September 2nd 1876, "I regard Custer's Massacre as a sacrifice of troops, brought on by Custer himself , that was wholly unnecessary-wholly unnecessary."

Like Lincoln, Custer has secured his place in history. His failure is worth examining to understand and apply to whatever position of leadership a person may enjoy.

JIM JONES AND THE PEOPLES CHURCH

Jim Jones was a charismatic leader, with a natural ability to influence others. Jones founded what would later become the Peoples Temple in 1954 and claimed as many as 20,000 members in the late '70s. In the beginning, there were what would generally be accepted as "good" intentions, but in the later years became a cult after moving from Indiana to the San Francisco area.

In 1974 the Temple leased land Near Georgetown in Guyana South America and began to move a core group to that location in the early '70s. After an exposé of Temple activities, Jones quickly moved along with a number of the congregation to Guyana to avoid further scurrility. The total of Temple members, including Jones, was about 900 or so.

On 17 November, 1978, Congressman Leo Ryan flew to Guyana to investigate the possibility of abuse in the Temple and to verify rumors that a number of the church wanted to leave but were prevented from doing so. The next day, Ryan brought a small number of Temple members to his plane to return to the US when they were attacked by Temple security guards, killing Ryan, three journalists, one of the defecting Temple members and injuring nine others.

The evening of the attack, Jones convinced most of the member of the Temple in Guyana to "drink the Kool-Aid" and 918 people died, including 276 children. A recording, available on the internet, of the moments where Temple members began drinking the poison lasts for about twenty minutes or so until there is, at last, nothing but the silence of the surrounding jungle. Jones can be heard encouraging those with small children to "help" them drink the poison.

Jones may have been one of the most effective leaders in that he was able to convince others that his purpose was a "greater good" even to the point where they were willing to take their own life and murder their children. His story is worth studying if only to understand how leadership can be twisted into something very evil.

PERSONAL EXAMPLES OF GOOD AND NOT SO VERY GOOD LEADERSHIP

The new commander. Towards the end of the Viet Nam War, this author was recently commissioned and placed on orders to attend Field Artillery Officers Basic or OBC. The course was designed to provide a working knowledge of the various complex pieces that comprise a Field Artillery unit. Upon reporting to Fort Sill, Oklahoma, several hundred brand new officers from around the country assembled, and the Army, as is its custom, structured the class into a battalion and then further divided into batteries (specific to the artillery and called companies in most other units, and platoons). The structure was very useful to manage the complicated training structure.

The new officers had come from many different sources; some had been enlisted soldiers that rose to the challenge of Officers Candidate School, commonly known as OCS, others graduated from Reserve Officers Training Courses from any one of a number of university programs, and others were the product of United States Military Academy at West Point. The battalion, battery and platoon leaders were selected and primarily were West Point graduates, the elite chosen few that were at the top of their class in high school and many had received their appointments to West Point through their state senator's office.

Our newly designated Battery Commander immediately began issuing orders as if he had some real authority, which technically he had. Unfortunately, there is so much more to leadership than issuing orders and he soon found himself in an uncomfortable position when his peers pushed back against his style. The one thing this newly minted leader failed to do was to gain permission from those he led to actually occupy that command position.

Permission to lead is conferred upon those that demonstrate several important attributes, the first of which is humility. This brand new leader missed an opportunity to become familiar with those of the same rank under his command; to understand who was under his command and who may have been, in fact, a unit leader prior to being placed on orders to OBC. Had he taken just a few minutes to understand who he was leading he would have been much better accepted in the position he was given. He would have discovered that he had combat veterans in the group and that he had former Sergeant's with leadership experience. Over time, he could have cultivated relationships and others could have gained confidence in his authority.

An acknowledgement up front that he did not have the gravity, or gravitas in political speak, to warrant the position he held would have saved some awkward moments later on. Fortunately, this particular gentleman was able to recover from his errors and eventually gained the respect of his peers who also happened to be his nominal subordinates. He also learned that leadership positions can also be lonely and require hard choices that affect the lives of others.

After a few rough bumps in my personal leadership road, I began to understand that time taken to visit with everyone on my new team was time well spent. In this case, "visit" was an introduction and opportunity to listen. Questions like, What do you think about…? Do you have all the tools you need to…? Are there policies and procedures I should look at to improve…?

The few days and weeks of a new leadership assignment are a golden opportunity to understand the makeup of the team and begin to understand who they are and what they really need from the team leader.

The carpenter. Mike was an excellent craftsman and finish carpenter with beautiful, customer pleasing results. As so often happens, a project superintendent's position opened up and Mike was tapped to fill the new job opening because of the great work and skilled craftsmanship.

Mike had no formal training for the new leadership role, but the boss was so impressed with his skills that he was certain the leadership element of the work would come naturally. Mike was uncertain, but not wanting to admit that he had finally encountered a challenge that truly was frightening, Mike had difficulty leaving the crew behind and distancing himself from the friendships that he so enjoyed, and this made unpleasant conversations about tardiness or cell phone use at work almost impossible to have. He was able to hide the mounting problems from the boss for quite a while, but eventually realized that he was miserable in the leadership position, especially when contrasted with the pleasure he found while putting work in place.

The next choice was whether to continue in this unhappy experience, all the while knowing his performance was substandard, or to meet with his boss and request reassignment back to his old position. Unfortunately the second option seemed so unpleasant that he continued in a job he hated until he was terminated for poor performance.

Several mistakes were made with Mike. First, the boss decided that an expert in a given field indicated leadership capabilities. Second,

Mike did not fully understand the price he had to pay for leadership and let himself be convinced to take a job with a corresponding pay raise and a boost in stature in the company. Third, Mike was afraid to confront the hard fact that he was not the person for the job.

Many times when employees are terminated, they know it is coming and sometimes are actually relieved when they are fired. Unfortunately, the promotion-grace period-and realization of a mistake can take months or longer, and, while Mike suffered with indecision, the company also was damaged and had to regain the confidence of the remaining employees.

Mike's immediate supervisor had much of the blame for this particular failure. In this particular instance the boss did not do his homework and rather than going through time consuming interviews of multiple candidates, chose to short cut the hiring/promotion process at great cost to a good craftsman and to the company as a whole.

Promotion from within can be challenging for all involved. The team already knows the individual that has been chosen to lead; the good and the bad are already right out there for all to see. The advice here is much the same as for a new leader brought in from the outside. Take time to visit with the team and genially seek their advice and opinions of the direction a new leader should take. This may not always align with the marching orders from the boss so leaders have to be willing to say, "I've heard you, and we can address some of the issues brought to the table, however there are some that simply are outside my wheelhouse that I cannot influence, so what can I do, if anything, to make the thinks I cannot change more palatable?"

PERSONAL THOUGHTS ON A CAREER OF LEADERSHIP

This book is intended for those already in a position of leadership that want to examine more leadership tools that may assist in the difficult task of leading others. It is also intended for those that desire to lead others and may want a roadmap to consider in their particular situation. In either situation, the main purpose is to engender a desire to learn more, develop new skills, and to interact with subordinates and senior leaders alike so that all can see growth, development, compassion, and the courage necessary to warrant leading others.

Hopefully this handbook will add to a library that all leaders need in that we, all of us, become what we think about and what we read and learn. The second element critical to those that desire to advance in leadership rolls or who have been tapped for leadership, are the people that we meet and build relationships with; in fact leadership requires change within and sometimes externally with a change in those with whom we associate.

Consider this: being so in demand that you endure endless texts with questions or feel that you cannot leave your staff alone without fear of some egregious problem surfacing, you may not really be a leader. Leaders look for ways to tap into the skills of others, make certain they understand the desired end results and then provide guidance and oversight along the way. This is the "Velvet Glove" of true leadership that is a combination of a soft touch and firm grip on rare occasions when absolutely necessary. This is the hard work of leadership.

Leadership is a concept that has been very difficult to nail down; there have been a number of efforts to determine why some lead and others follow. Initially the thought was that leaders displayed certain traits such as intelligence, masculinity, and dominance. Unfortunately, these traits fail to account for the increasing numbers of effective female leaders that have ascended to national, corporate, and other organizations of various sizes and purposes.

One of the best leaders I personally worked for was a Chief Operating Officer, and RN, and former Air Force Officer. The COO I worked for was certainly intelligent, but her leadership style was certainly not one of dominance and masculinity. Looking back now through the lens of a decade or so, my perception was that she did not try to be something other than herself. LeAnn's style was very assertive but not overbearing, teaching with understanding, and very democratic.

I have also worked for, and have been, a leader that that was more autocratic and directive in nature than most. It is not fair, or correct, to say that all male leaders are ______ and all female leaders are ______, whatever term you would use to fill in the blank.

Men and women can succeed as leaders without becoming some androgynous personality; the secret is to build on their respective strengths. This is probably a good lesson for all those that aspire to leadership roles; don't try to be someone else or what you think others believe you should be. Understand yourself and, using some of the tools discussed elsewhere in this book, find your strengths and build on them and discover your weakness and work to improve those things that need improved.

This work is intended to study the pieces and parts of leadership from a perspective of a lifetime of leadership in small business, the military, volunteer organizations, academia, and the corporate world. Attributes of leadership will be examined and, hopefully, a desire to learn more about the various tools in a leader's toolbox. Together we will look at the roles of leaders and team members and we will look at how knowledge from both formal and informal education can impact a leader's performance. The intent is to provide some insight and some practical thought for those thrust into leadership, for those that desire to achieve a leadership position, and for existing leaders to consider as challenges present.

This is tough work to own all those pieces and parts of leadership style. Even harder is deploying those different styles in different leadership situations. I spent over thirty years in my first career in construction and concurrent with that, twenty-four years as a Field Artillery Officer in the National Guard. And then I pivoted to a job that eventually allowed me to contribute to the management of more than 30 billion in healthcare assets in a Fortune 50 company.

It was a culture shock to move from make dominated fields such as the military and construction to the female-dominated industry of healthcare. Fortunately for my own survival, my office in my first healthcare job as Director of Facilities in a medium sized hospital was in a separate building about a quarter mile from the main hospital. When I would get a call that initially seemed to me to be trivial, I would begin that five- or ten-minute walk to visit with the caller, usually a nurse in one of the various departments. The few moments of that walk saved me from myself many times as I saw the call initially as a rude interruption of my carefully planned day. Over the course of the walk, I would often reflect on the call and come to understand several very important things about the meeting I was soon to have.

My first challenge was to remember that I was no longer a Lt. Colonel in charge of a nuclear capable artillery battalion. In that particular assignment and depending on the urgency of the situation, my response tended to be rather abrupt and not necessarily displaying all of the desired leadership styles mentioned above. I also had to tamp down the direct communication style that I used as President and CEO of a Regional General Construction firm. What I initially saw as the inconvenience of having a remote office, became the salvation of my third career.

I was often surprised to find that I had an intimidating presence, but I simply did not see myself through the lens of others. My 6'1" and 220-pound frame was useful in my development of a command presence, but not so much in the presence of a 5'7" and 120-pound nurse (just a side note; our infection control nurse may have been 5' tall and 90 pounds when wet, but she terrified me! She was crusty, direct, and in your face when a mistake was made, so the lesson here is that physical presence is not always how you are perceived, but rather how you carry that presence that matters). There was no way that I could hide who I was, and it would not have been proper to attempt to be someone other than myself.

My walk gave me an opportunity to remind myself that I was meeting with someone to discuss something very important to them, even if my perception was that the problem was just not that big of a deal. Those few moments helped me to remember to relax, and while I was never able to escape the command presence developed in a lifetime of leadership, to incorporate as best I could the styles appropriate to those relationships in my healthcare job, I actually learned how to smile and to get others to relax and visit. Initially it was a challenge to take the time to visit about family, to adopt a more relaxed posture, and to understand it was beneficial to really listen to what they had to say in a peer-to-peer discussion.

The bottom line is that you are who you are, but there are certain personal aspects that can change to adapt to the necessities of leadership. Take the time to attempt to see yourself as others see you. Seek advice on how different people require different approaches, and look at how your body language may speak louder than your words.

Regular folks like you and I can be called to lead. In fact, the military, in its incessant need to generate new generations of leaders, maintains that almost anyone can learn leadership and they are largely correct in that belief.

BIBLIOGRAPHY

Kinicki, Angelo, and Robert Kreitner. 2003. *Orgabizational Behavior*. Edited by john Weimeister. New York: McGraw-Hill.

RECOMMENDED READING

Do's and Taboos Around the World by Roger E. Axtell, *The Deming Management Method*, by Mary Walton
The Art of Writing Effective Letters by Fruehling and Bouchard
On-line resources
www.16personalities.com
Wikeapedia to learn more about Heros and Goats